DATE DUE			
Mar 26 76			
Apr 25 '80			
Nov 13 '80			

GERMANY
its geography and growth

GERMANY

its geography and growth

Karl A. Sinnhuber

Reader in Geography, University of Surrey

JOHN MURRAY   FIFTY ALBEMARLE STREET   LONDON

Preface and Acknowledgements

Geographical books—if taken in the widest sense—usually fall into two main categories: those read for pleasure and those used as sources of reference or as textbooks. This book was intended to be a bit of both and, judging by the comments of reviewers, readers and colleagues, it succeeded to a larger extent than the author dared hope. By adding a section of colour photographs and expanding the text the author and publisher attempt with this second edition to come even closer to this dual goal: to bring pleasure and to inform. Other changes include a thorough revision of the text to take account of developments since 1960 and the replacement of many photographs. To all those persons, firms and organisations listed below who supplied photographs author and publisher express their gratitude. The author also wishes to thank Inter Nationes, Bad Godesberg, for their assistance in the preparation of the colour section, the Audio-Visual Aids Unit of the University of Surrey for producing from the author's own photographs and colour slides prints which were suitable as a basis for reproduction; he wishes to repeat his indebtedness to the members of the drawing unit of the Department of Geography, University College London, for drawing the maps and diagrams retained from the first edition. The relief base and drainage pattern of the topographic maps were supplied by Geographische Anstalt Karl Wenschow, GmbH., München.

The sources of photographs are as follows (t, *top*; b, *bottom*; r, *right*; l, *left*; c, *centre*; roman numerals refer to Colour Section):

Author, on pp. 29b, 43r, 100b, 101t, 102, 106t, 109tc and b, 112r, 120l, 121l, 122r, 123, 124, 125t, 126, It, IItl, III, VII, VIII, X, XI.
Adam Opel A.G. Rüsselsheim (Photograph, Aero-Lux, Frankfurt/M.), on p. Vtl.
A.G. für Berg-und Hüttenbetriebe, Salzgitter, on p. 51t.
Dr D. Beckmann, Giessen, on p. IItr.
Bundesbildstelle, Bonn, on pp. 9, 10, 17, 23b, 24, 29t, 54l, 56, 59, 60, 61tl, 67t and br, 81tr, 82, 83bc, 89r, 90tl and bl, 93b, 100t, 117, 120r.
Burda Bilderdienst, Offenburg, on pp. XIV, XVI.
Deutsche Luftbild K.G., Hamburg, on p. IVt.
Deutsche Shell A.G. (Photograph Hanseatische Luftfoto GmbH.), on p. 62t.
Deutsche Zentrale für Fremdenverkehr, Frankfurt/M., on pp. Vtr, VI, IX.
Farbenfabriken Bayer, A.G. Leverkusen, on p. IIb.
Friedrich Krupp, Stabsabteilung Information, Essen, on p. 55.
Georg Westermann Verlag, Braunschweig, on p. XIIt.
German Tourist Information Bureau, London, on pp. 2, 11, 14, 15, 16, 19, 23t, 25l, 26l, 27, 28, 32, 35, 36, 37, 39, 43l, 44, 45tr and l, 46, 47b, 48, 49l, 50, 54r, 58, 61r and bl, 62b, 63, 66, 67bl, 68, 69, 70, 71, 72, 73, 75, 76, 77, 78, 79, 80, 81tl and br, 83r and l, 85, 86, 87, 88, 89l, 90tr and br, 91, 92, 93t, 105t, br and bl, 106b, 107tr and b.
Gesellschaft für kulturelle Verbindungen mit dem Ausland, Berlin (East), on pp. 97, 101b, 103, 105c, 107tl, 109t and bc, 110, 111, 112l, 113, 114, 116, XIIb.
Herder Verlag, Freiburg, on pp. Vb, XIII, XV.
Keystone Press Agency Ltd, London, on pp. 21.
Landesbildstelle Niedersachsen, Hannover, on p. 45br.
Landesbildstelle Württemberg, Stuttgart, on p. 26r.
Luftbildtechnik, Berlin (West), on p. 47t.
Neue Heimat, Gemeinnützige Wohnungs-und Siedlungsgesellschaft mbH., Hamburg (Photograph, Deutsche Luftbild K.G., Hamburg), on p. Ib.
Plan und Karte, GmbH., Münster, on pp. 25r, 95, 96, 121r, 122l.
Press Department, Ministry of Foreign Affairs of the German Democratic Republic, Berlin (East), on pp. 104, 115.
H. Saebens, Worpswede, on p. 125b.
Schöning & Co., Lübeck, on p. 49r.
Staatsbibliothek Berlin, Bildarchiv, on p. 7.
Volkswagenwerk, A.G., Wolfsburg, on p. 51b.

First published 1961
Second edition 1970
Reprinted 1971

Main text printed by Jarrold & Sons Ltd, Norwich. Colour section printed by R. Müller, Köln-Braunsfeld. Bound by Jarrold & Sons.
0 7195 1286 7 (trade edition) 0 7195 1287 5 (school edition)

Contents

**Situated almost at the centre of the land hemisphere—the circle marks
the location of Berlin—Germany is ideally suited for trading. The present
division of the world into two main political camps and the division of
Germany itself have, however, largely eliminated this advantage.**

PART ONE

A Panoramic View

GERMANY—WHAT DOES IT MEAN?

THE EVOLUTION OF GERMANY

PHYSIQUE

CLIMATE

Germany is justly known as "the country of poets and philosophers". Although it has other remarkable achievements to its credit, there is no doubt that the greatest German contributions to civilisation lie in the fields of literature, philosophy and music. Two out of many thinkers and writers, Goethe and Schiller, who were closely associated with the city of Weimar where this monument stands, certainly belong to all mankind.

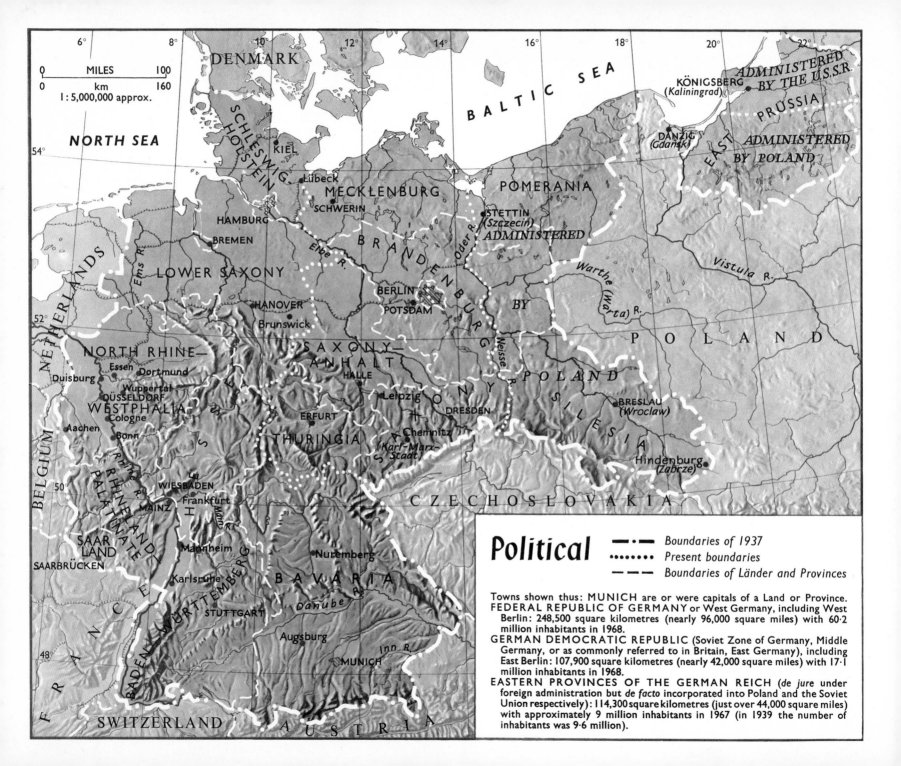

NORTH SEA

BALTIC SEA

DENMARK

SCHLESWIG-HOLSTEIN
KIEL
Lübeck

MECKLENBURG
SCHWERIN

POMERANIA
STETTIN (Szczecin)
ADMINISTERED

KÖNIGSBERG (Kaliningrad)

ADMINISTERED BY THE U.S.S.R.

EAST PRUSSIA
DANZIG (Gdansk)
ADMINISTERED BY POLAND

NETHERLANDS

HAMBURG
BREMEN

Ems R.
Elbe R.

LOWER SAXONY

BRANDENBURG
Oder R.

HANOVER
Brunswick

BERLIN
POTSDAM

BY

Warthe (Warta) R.

Vistula R.

NORTH RHINE-
Essen   Dortmund
Duisburg
Wuppertal
DÜSSELDORF
WESTPHALIA
Cologne
Aachen   Bonn

SAXONY-ANHALT
HALLE
Leipzig

Neisse R.

POLAND

POLAND

SILESIA
BRESLAU (Wroclaw)

BELGIUM

Rhine R.
RHINELAND-PALATINATE

THURINGIA
ERFURT

Chemnitz (Karl-Marx-Stadt)
DRESDEN

Hindenburg (Zabrze)

WIESBADEN
MAINZ
Frankfurt
Main R.

SAAR LAND
SAARBRÜCKEN

Mannheim

HESSE

CZECHOSLOVAKIA

FRANCE

Karlsruhe
BADEN-WÜRTTEMBERG
STUTTGART

Nuremberg

BAVARIA

Danube R.

Augsburg

MUNICH

Inn R.

SWITZERLAND

AUSTRIA

Political

—·—	Boundaries of 1937
••••••	Present boundaries
— — —	Boundaries of Länder and Provinces

Towns shown thus: MUNICH are or were capitals of a Land or Province.
FEDERAL REPUBLIC OF GERMANY or West Germany, including West Berlin: 248,500 square kilometres (nearly 96,000 square miles) with 60·2 million inhabitants in 1968.
GERMAN DEMOCRATIC REPUBLIC (Soviet Zone of Germany, Middle Germany, or as commonly referred to in Britain, East Germany), including East Berlin: 107,900 square kilometres (nearly 42,000 square miles) with 17·1 million inhabitants in 1968.
EASTERN PROVINCES OF THE GERMAN REICH (*de jure* under foreign administration but *de facto* incorporated into Poland and the Soviet Union respectively): 114,300 square kilometres (just over 44,000 square miles) with approximately 9 million inhabitants in 1967 (in 1939 the number of inhabitants was 9·6 million).

Apart from "The Wall" in Berlin, no boundary could be more inhuman and contrary to all geographical principles than the section of the "Iron Curtain" which runs through the heart of Germany dividing neighbours and families and separating farmers from their fields. Although on the whole it follows previously existing internal administrative boundaries, these were of little significance in the daily life of the people. The course of this boundary was originally agreed amongst the Allied Powers as early as November 1944, but its purpose was merely to be a demarcation line between the Soviet Zone of Occupation and those of the United States and the United Kingdom. Although *de jure* it is still a demarcation line and is in West Germany called the "Zonal Boundary", with the hardened division of Germany it has in practice become a state boundary. Its length from the Baltic Sea to the westernmost tip of Czechoslovakia is nearly 1,400 kilometres. Of the 32 railway lines, 3 motorways and 171 public roads which were cut by it when it came into being, only 10 railway lines, the motorways and 2 roads are still open to traffic; the others were blocked up and have become overgrown, as shown in this picture. While on the western side one may go right up to the boundary fence, there is on the eastern side a zone of 5 kilometres which may only be entered by residents and others with a special permit. The boundary is followed by electrified barbed-wire, an 11-metres wide ploughed and raked strip, and a system of watch-towers. It is closely guarded by frontier police who will shoot without warning if anyone should enter this forbidden strip. In this way and by the rides which have been cut where it runs through forests, the unhappy division of Germany is immediately geographically observable.

1. Germany—what does it mean?

What does this title indicate? It is not easy to give a short answer to this question for "Germany" defies simple definition.

When we speak of the United Kingdom, or almost any other country, there is no doubt what we mean by it; it is in every case a state with clear boundaries, and there is no other of the same name. But there is now no state which is simply called Germany. The country was divided as a consequence of the Second World War and the occupation of Germany by the troops of the Allied Powers.

First there is West Germany or, to give it its official name, the Federal Republic of Germany. It extends over the areas which were from 1945 to 1955 the American, British and French zones of occupation; this is the largest of the parts into which Germany came to be divided.

But when we speak of the geography of Germany we must deal with a larger area, despite the fact that some parts now lie behind the "Iron Curtain". We must include Berlin and what was the Soviet Zone of Occupation. This too has become a state, the German Democratic Republic. However, although it is now after the Soviet Union economically most important within the Soviet bloc, its government still obeys the wishes of the Soviet leaders with such eagerness that there is, in practice, little difference from its previous status. Indeed only in 1969 was it given full diplomatic recognition by any other than Communist states.

This second major part of Germany, which is considerably smaller than the Federal Republic, is outside Germany often called "East Germany". This is geographically speaking a misnomer and the regional term used instead in this book is "Middle Germany". The reason is that *geographically* Germany does not end at the eastern boundary of the G.D.R., which is formed by two rivers, the Oder and its tributary the Neisse. Eastwards of these rivers lie

the ancient provinces of Pomerania, East Prussia, Silesia and the eastern part of Brandenburg.

This third major part of Germany was in 1945 put under Polish and Soviet administration according to the Potsdam Agreement concluded between the United Kingdom, the United States and the Soviet Union. Today few Germans still live there, since most were expelled to start a new life west of the Oder–Neisse. Yet one would not do justice to geographical realities if these "lost provinces" were omitted. The geographer's main concern is not with political boundaries and states; it is with landscapes and regions which he has to describe and interpret. These have taken a long time to develop and many generations of people have shaped them. For more than five centuries these provinces were inhabited by Germans, who have left their mark on the landscape. Whatever its new inhabitants may have done in the last decades to alter the face of the land, most of its features are still of German origin and thus of German character.

Even if we ignored the appearance of the landscape and defined "Germany" strictly by reference to political boundaries, the eastern provinces would still have to be included. The Oder–Neisse line, though *de facto* the western boundary of Poland, has not the legal status of an internationally recognised frontier. According to the Potsdam Agreement it was to be the demarcation line between the Soviet Occupation Zone and the German provinces under Polish administration. Only through a peace treaty can it acquire *de jure* status as repeated demands by Soviet leaders for such a treaty "to give legal status to these territorial changes" clearly show.

Throughout history there have been changes in the political boundaries of Germany. There were times when Germany was split up into so many territories that it was no more than a geographical expression. As a geographical region, however, it persisted; and it is historic Germany, *Germany as a region* rather than a state, which is the subject of this book. To try to understand what it is like today, and why it has become so, we have to look back at its development, its growth. But "growth" does not imply merely the extension of national boundaries; it means rather a growing understanding of how best to use the natural endowment of the country, how to improve the partnership between man and nature. To explain, in outline, how this is achieved; to point out the major geographical problems of Germany; to indicate the great variety of its landscapes—these are the main objects of this book.

More than two decades have passed since the war ended, but the shells of bombed buildings still remain in many German towns. Eventually most will disappear, but some, like the tower of the Emperor William Memorial Church in Berlin, have been preserved in their ruined state—in the words of a bronze plaque on its north wall, ". . . as a memento of God's punishment that befell the German people in the years of the War."

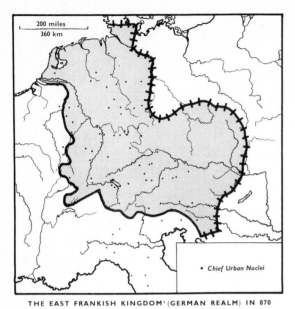

THE EAST FRANKISH KINGDOM (GERMAN REALM) IN 870   THE HOLY ROMAN EMPIRE OF THE GERMAN NATION IN 1250   EASTWARD EXPANSION OF GERMAN SETTLEMENT

2. The evolution of Germany

Everyone knows how swiftly and how greatly the boundaries of a state may alter in the course of its history. Geographical regions change more slowly, but change they do. It is therefore necessary at the outset to realise how the geographical unit which we have just termed "Germany" varied in size and shape over the centuries. The process, as we shall see, has not been merely one of gradual expansion; the historical development was at times reversed and certain areas which were once part of "Germany" (such as Austria, Switzerland or even the Netherlands) have become attached elsewhere or have emerged as units in their own right.

The first political unit which may be considered the direct ancestor of present-day Germany, although it did not bear this

name, came into being over a thousand years ago when, in 843, the grandsons of Charles the Great (or Charlemagne) divided the Frankish Empire into three—a western part, predominantly Latin, an eastern part, largely Teutonic, and a central area, lying between these two realms, which was linguistically mixed. Most of this latter kingdom, which came to be called "Lotharingia" (from which the name of the French province "Lorraine" is derived) after its first ruler, went to the eastern, i.e. German, realm in further partitions in 870 and 887, but the effects of the original tripartition were felt for centuries afterwards. The struggle to rule this middle part runs as a major and constantly recurring theme through the histories of Germany and France, bedevilling relations

GERMANY IN 1807

| | Prussian Kingdom | | Rhenish Confederation | | Austrian Empire |

GERMANY IN 1815–66

| | Prussian Kingdom | | Austrian Empire | — | Boundary of German Confederation |

THE GERMAN REICH 1871 (TO 1918)

| | North German Confederation | | South German States | | Alsace-Lorraine |

between them. It is only during recent years that Germany and France have, by mutual give-and-take, achieved an understanding so that now there is hope that this age-old struggle will never be resumed.

The earliest "Germany", the German realm which resulted from the division of the Carolingian Empire, was ruled, more in name than in fact, by Lewis the German and his descendants until the male line became extinct in 911. The actual power lay in the hands of the dukes, the rulers of the different German tribes. The Frankish rulers who had so long enjoyed supremacy now had to give way to a Saxon, Henry the Fowler, who was elected king, and it was this Saxon House which ushered in Germany's period of greatness in the Middle Ages. The pressure upon the German peoples by the Slavs and the Magyars from the East gave real authority to this ruler of the German realm, but it was left to his son, Otto I (the Great), to consolidate this authority and weld Germany into what was, by medieval standards, a well-organised state. Having assumed the Italian crown and decisively defeated the Magyars in 955, he held a position of greater influence and prestige than any other ruler since Charles the Great. It was quite natural that he, like Charles, should be crowned Roman Emperor in Rome. This event in 962 marks the establishment of the Holy Roman Empire of the German Nation.

At the time of Charles the Great, the divide between the Teutonic

The imperial palace in Goslar built in the tenth century. The Holy Roman Empire of the German Nation had no definite capital. There were instead a number of these palaces or Pfalzen where the Emperor held court from time to time.

in the Austrian Habsburgs, the process of its disintegration had gone too far to be reversed or even halted.

The Reformation split the German nation further on religious lines, a cleavage which culminated in the civil strife of the Thirty Years War (1618–48). This sad spectacle was repeated during the eighteenth century and again during the Napoleonic Wars. When in 1806 Francis II renounced the title of Holy Roman Emperor and styled himself Emperor of Austria instead, he merely acknowledged a state of affairs dating back at least to the Thirty Years War: that the Holy Roman Empire and a united Germany, which had begun with so much promise in the tenth century, had ceased to exist.

Other consequences arose from the establishment by Henry the Fowler and Otto I of the eastern marches. This marked the beginning of the expansion eastwards of the area of the German settlement into mainly Slav lands, hitherto thinly settled. Usually this expansion was a peaceful process, as in Silesia, Bohemia and Hungary where the German settlers were invited by the native rulers. Occasionally it was preceded by fierce fighting, particularly in East Prussia, where the Order of the Teutonic Knights was engaged in a "life or death" struggle with the heathen tribe of the Prussi. But in either case the settlers came from all over Germany, even from as far as Flanders, and transformed primeval woodlands and swamps into flourishing agricultural tracts. The Germans also came as pioneers of mining, and as craftsmen and merchants; and they founded numerous towns and cities which became centres of trade and civilisation. When this process of eastward migration ceased in the fifteenth century the German-speaking area had nearly doubled in extent, and beyond the distinctively German area there were many "islands" of German speech, extending as far as the eastern Baltic shores in the north and Transylvania in the south-east. The centre of gravity of Germany, which had been the Rhinelands, had shifted eastwards: it is significant to note that the first German university was founded at Prague and the second at Vienna.

peoples and the Slavs had run approximately along the Elbe and Saale rivers to the Bohemian Forest and the River Enns in the Alps. The following century had seen Slavs and Magyars advance westwards. The reigns of Henry and Otto mark the turning of the tide. Henry successfully defended the eastern frontier and Otto even pushed it farther east, establishing a string of marches (in German: *Marken*) and also obtaining the overlordship of Bohemia and Moravia. His achievements had many important consequences.

The imperial crown proved a mixed blessing. Though it gave the ruler of Germany an enhanced status, he became involved in Italy, and the attempts, ultimately futile, to retain his overlordship there sapped the Empire's strength and gradually but steadily diminished the power of the Emperor over the dukes and the other territorial rulers in Germany. The title of Holy Roman Emperor became in time no more than honorific—a process which was furthered by the fact that the monarchy was elective, so that no ruling house had the chance of establishing itself firmly. When at last the Empire found a centre in Vienna and an enduring dynasty

By 1500 the outlines of the linguistic map of Middle and Eastern Europe had been established and there was relatively little change for over four centuries. When, as a result of the Second World War, change did come it was sudden and tremendous. It is true that after the First World War a number of Germans left those territories which had fallen to Poland, but it was the Second World War that started a German exodus of unbelievable magnitude.

Hitler, the dictator of Germany from 1933 to 1945, took the first step when in 1939 he arranged a transfer westwards of the German-speaking peoples from the Baltic states, eastern Poland and the southern Ukraine; the next step came towards the close of the war when the Red Army advanced into Germany and many German settlers, forsaking all their possessions, fled with the retreating German forces. The major and final event which contracted the German-speaking area to not much more than the area it had occupied under Otto the Great, a thousand years before, came after the war. This was the expulsion of almost all the German-speaking people, regardless of whether or not they had been German nationals, from the areas east of the Oder–Neisse line, from Czechoslovakia, Hungary and Yugoslavia. In all, probably as many as 17 million people were uprooted from the lands to which their ancestors had come hundreds of years before.

But to return once more to the time of Henry the Fowler and Otto the Great. From the establishment of the eastern marches resulted a change not only in the cultural but also the political centre of gravity. Two of these marchlands were to become of the utmost importance for Germany's destiny, the Eastern March (*Ostmark*; *Österreich*, which means the eastern realm) around which evolved the Austro-Hungarian Empire, and the Northern March which became the nucleus of the powerful state of Prussia. At first mere dependent counties, they emancipated themselves, gained territories and became a kingdom (Prussia) and an archduchy (Austria). To the latter were also added the crowns of Bohemia and Hungary in 1526.

It was Austria which first achieved the leading position within

The town hall of Osnabrück is of great significance in the history of Germany. It was there that the treaty of 1648 was signed concluding the terrible Thirty Years War. Many towns and whole provinces lay devastated and the population losses were so great that it took a century to make them good.

Germany. The date which marks the rise of Austria to major importance is the year 1282 when Rudolph, the first Habsburg emperor, entrusted the duchy, whose ruling house had died out, to his sons, thus starting the rule of the House of Habsburg which was to last until the end of the First World War in 1918.

We need not concern ourselves in detail with the growth of Austrian importance nor with its territorial gains and losses over the centuries. That it had risen to the leading role is illustrated by the fact that from 1438 onward, except for an interval of a mere three years, the rulers of Austria also wore the imperial crown of the Holy Roman Empire. True, Austria suffered set-backs during the Thirty Years War, but it was another hundred years before it was successfully challenged by another German power, Brandenburg-Prussia; and it took a further hundred years to decide the struggle for leadership within Germany, with Prussia emerging victorious.

The rise to importance of the Northern March came later than that of the Eastern March. Founded in the tenth century, it gradually extended and by the middle of the twelfth century had become the Margraviate of Brandenburg. A further increase in status occurred when, a century later, its ruler was raised to the rank of Elector, i.e. one of the rulers with the right to elect the Holy Roman Emperor. One fact, however, is of outstanding importance in the story of the emergence of Brandenburg (or, as it later became, Prussia) as the leading German power. This was the accession of a new ruling house, the Hohenzollern, in 1411. A major change came just before the outbreak of the Thirty Years War when some small territories on the lower reaches of the Rhine, as well as the Duchy of East Prussia, became attached to Brandenburg. The Thirty Years War prevented any effective consolidation of these new gains, but in the peace that followed Brandenburg emerged with a further increase of territory as the most important of the German states which had accepted the new Lutheran faith. In 1701 its ruler assumed the title of King of Prussia and in 1740, with the accession of Frederick II (the Great), Prussia was ready to challenge Austria.

Austria, to the throne of which Maria Theresa had succeeded in

The equestrian statue of Frederick William, the Great Elector, who after the Thirty Years War laid the foundations of Prussia's rise to power. The monument, by Schlüter, now standing in the forecourt of Schloss Charlottenburg in Berlin, is one of the most important sculptures of German Baroque art.

No other place, not even Berlin, is associated so much with the history of Brandenburg-Prussia as is Potsdam, "the Prussian Versailles". Of its many palaces, none is more charming than Sans Souci for which Frederick the Great himself sketched the plans. It became his favourite residence and he died there in 1786. This and Schloss Cecilienhof, where the Potsdam conference was held, are major tourist attractions.

the same year, was taken by surprise when Frederick invaded Silesia in 1740. The real strength of Prussia became apparent, however, in the Seven Years War (1756–63). Prussia, surrounded by powerful enemies on all sides—Austria, Russia, France and Sweden—and with England as her only ally, was finally victorious, though many times nearly defeated. Little wonder that Austria resented this and that further battles were to reopen the struggle.

Before this happened an outside force, in the person of Napoleon, took a hand in Germany's fate. Fighting partly together, partly independently, Austria and Prussia suffered a series of defeats and territorial losses. Most of the states of western Germany formed the Confederation of the Rhine and supported Napoleon; it was because of this that Francis II decided to abandon the title of Holy Roman Emperor. The tide turned when Napoleon over-reached himself in Russia in 1812. The German War of Liberation followed. Prussia and then Austria joined the Allies against Napoleon, and after his crushing defeat at Leipzig in 1813 even

the states of the Confederation of the Rhine turned against him. But military victory was not all. For the first time since the defence of the eastern frontier during the Middle Ages, all Germans, though split up into many states, joined in a common cause. From this united action, and from the fervent writings of poets and philosophers, German nationalism was born, aiming at the creation of a unified state with boundaries embracing all the German-speaking peoples. This popular dream came to nothing. Austria, as the strongest German power, had become more and more involved in south-eastern Europe, into which it had expanded and was too preoccupied to assume the leadership of a new German Empire. Prussia, on the other hand, was not yet ready for such leadership, even if Austria had been prepared to acquiesce.

The changes brought about by this wave of popular nationalism were feeble enough. A loose Confederation of the German states, now numbering 39 instead of the 360 or so which had existed before the rise of Napoleon, was set up under the presidency of

Austria. In failing to satisfy the German people, the Confederation carried its own death-warrant from the beginning. It was a lingering death, however, taking nearly fifty years. The individual rulers wanted no change and, with the support of the police and army, spared no efforts to maintain the *status quo*. Nevertheless, the fire of nationalism continued to smoulder and in the spring of 1848 it broke into flames. Within a few weeks there were revolutions in almost all the German states. A German parliament met in Frankfurt-on-Main with the aim of establishing a truly national union. Again these hopes came to nothing. After much debate a draft constitution was passed, and in recognition that Austria, too involved with its south-eastern problems, was unable to assume the leadership, the imperial crown was offered in 1849 to the King of Prussia. But he refused it. A golden opportunity was missed, the sovereigns of the various states regained command, and popular feeling was once more frustrated.

When unity did come, it was only partial and by consent of the rulers. The first move in this direction had already taken place some time previously in the sphere of economics. This was the establishment of three customs unions in 1828, and in 1834 the creation of the *Zollverein*, a customs union which was gradually joined by almost all German states, but from which Austria was excluded on the insistence of Prussia. Political unification of the states of the *Zollverein* under Prussian leadership was, however, impossible as long as Austria occupied the presidency of the German Confederation. To realise this and eventually to satisfy the desire for German unity, though it was a unity which left the Germans of Austria outside the fold, was largely the work of one man, Otto von Bismarck, who became Prime Minister of Prussia in 1862. He was convinced that German unity could not be achieved by speeches and resolutions but by "blood and iron", a phrase which became famous and earned him the name of "The Iron Chancellor".

The first action for which Bismarck was responsible was, however, undertaken jointly with Austria. In 1864 they wrested the German provinces of Schleswig and Holstein from the King of Denmark, who had attempted to integrate them more fully in his country. Disagreement with Austria over the administration of these provinces provided the necessary pretext for Bismarck's next step. In 1866 Austria and Prussia went to war—a war which lasted only six weeks and in which Prussia was successful from the start. The conditions imposed on Austria in the peace treaty were very moderate. Bismarck had achieved his object; Austria had been ousted from the leadership of Germany, and he did not wish to inflict humiliation and to create bitter resentment. Austria ceded no territory to Prussia, but had to recognise Prussia's right to establish a North German Confederation and to annex a number of north German territories, so that Prussia, for the first time in history, formed a continuous stretch of land from the western frontiers of Germany to its boundary with Russia.

The next and final step to establish the German Reich came only three years later, in 1870. Bismarck was convinced that France would not agree to a unification of Germany and that war was inevitable. Relations between Prussia and France became strained in 1870 over the question of the succession to the throne of Spain; and as Bismarck had expected, and hoped, France declared war on Prussia. It was again a *Blitzkrieg* in which the decisive battles were fought in little more than six weeks. The French "Second Empire" collapsed, and on 18 January 1871, the history of the "Second Reich" began when, in the Hall of Mirrors at Versailles, King William of Prussia was acclaimed German Emperor by all the rulers of the German states—except Austria, which stayed outside this "Little Germany".

The peace treaty with France was less moderate than that with Austria. France had to cede Alsace and Lorraine, and pay substantial reparations; the treaty thus created the desire for revenge, the opportunity for which was not to come until 1918. Meanwhile the German Empire reached the peak of its power.

For centuries "Germany" had been no more than a geographical expression; the new nation-state quickly made up for lost time, ascending to a position of world importance, politically as well as economically. It underwent tremendous economic development and, at the cost of straining Anglo-German relations, acquired colonies in Africa and the Pacific and built a large fleet. But not all was well behind this display of might and prosperity. The Reich had come not as the result of a popular movement but on the basis of an agreement between the rulers. There was no genuine democratic government and the contrast in status between landowner and agricultural labourer, industrial baron and worker, was very great. There was further the question of national minorities; Poles in the east, Danes in North Schleswig, and the inhabitants of Alsace and Lorraine who—though largely German-speaking—were treated harshly and were therefore hostile to German rule. In Germany's relation with other countries, too, there were shortcomings. Germany's foreign policy aroused suspicion and fear in most of the neighbouring countries, especially after Bismarck had been made to resign in 1890 by the new Kaiser, William II. The result was that by the end of 1905 Germany was almost completely isolated, except for the support of Austria. Europe was divided into two camps feverishly arming against each other, and one crisis followed another. Under the circumstances it was inevitable that there should be one crisis too many. This came with the assassination in 1914 of the Austrian Archduke in Sarajevo. Austria was determined to chastise Serbia for this outrage and the Kaiser gave his assent. He must have known that this action was bound to start a general European war.

We need not concern ourselves here with the course of the First World War. It was fought with immense losses on both sides and the end in 1918 brought not only

Saint Paul's church in Frankfurt-on-Main where the first all-German parliament met in May 1848 with the aim of achieving a union of the German states. Although this assembly contained some of the finest characters and noblest minds in Germany, it had no real power, and failed. In the words of the historian, A. J. P. Taylor, 1848 was the year when German history reached its turning-point and failed to turn.

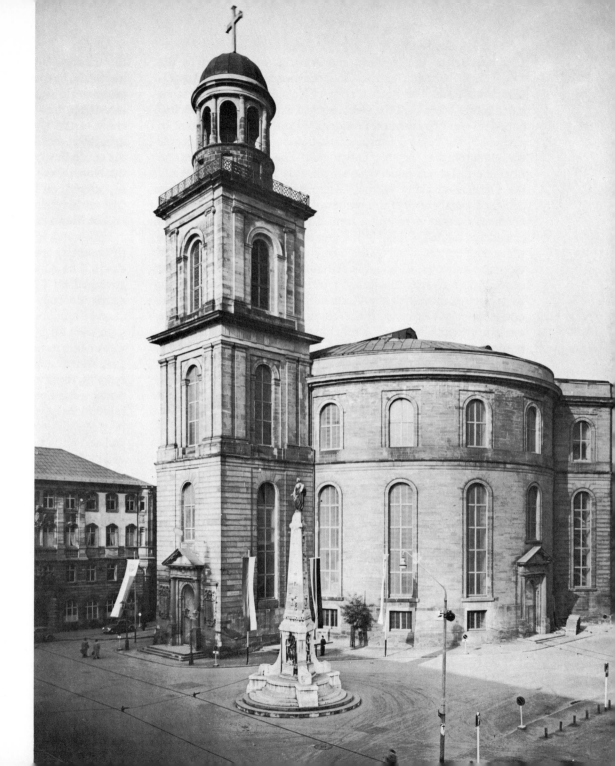

complete defeat to Germany and Austria, but an end of the monarchies in both countries and the break-up of the Austro-Hungarian state. The Peace Treaty of Versailles turned out to be much more severe than the Germans had expected, since they had hoped it would be based on President Wilson's fourteen points. In particular, the point concerning self-determination of the people was not applied as they had anticipated. The return of Alsace and Lorraine to France came as no surprise. If Danzig (Gdansk) and the German-speaking Memel (Klaipeda) district had not been detached clearly against the wishes of the inhabitants, the loss of northern Schleswig resulting from a plebiscite would have been considered as just. Probably the greatest disappointment was the transfer of eastern Upper Silesia to Poland despite a plebiscite in Germany's favour. Although it fell outside the letter of the point concerning self-determination, the refusal to allow the Austrian Republic to unite with the German state and the denial of the option to join Germany to the ethnically German people, who made up the majority of the inhabitants of that part of Bohemia bordering Germany and Austria, was nevertheless felt to be contrary to the spirit of the principle. How right President Wilson was when he wrote that an imposed settlement "would leave a sting . . . upon which terms of peace would rest, not permanently, but only as upon quicksand".

There is no doubt that the resentment against the "dictate of Versailles", as it came to be called, was widespread and deep and provided fuel to the rise of German nationalism. The party which particularly exploited this, the idealism of the German youths and the despair of the millions of unemployed during the depression of the early 1930s, was the National Socialist (Nazi) Party under its *Führer*, Adolf Hitler. After being called upon to form a government in January 1933, Hitler quickly eliminated all other parties and succeeded over the next four years in tearing up the Treaty of Versailles as far as it concerned internal German matters. He then went beyond this and in 1938 brought Austria and the so-called Sudeten Provinces "home into the Reich" as the current slogan went. In spring 1939 he also established German control over the remainder of Czechoslovakia and the Memel district. After an agreement with Stalin on the division of the spheres of influence in East-central Europe, Adolf Hitler ordered, on 1 September 1939,

the invasion of Poland. At last Britain and France decided to intervene; he must have realised that the invasion of Poland would mean world war. Initially the well-prepared German forces were victorious, but when Hitler also attacked Russia, and after the entry of the United States into the war, Germany's defeat was inevitable, inevitable despite the German forces' control of nearly the entire European mainland from the Atlantic to the Volga, from the North Cape to Crete and a large part of North Africa as well. An attempt on Hitler's life in 1944 by a German resistance group was unsuccessful and the war in Europe was fought to its bitter end in May 1945.

Hitler and several of his closest associates committed suicide; the country, after unconditional surrender, was in a state of utter chaos. The Allies stated that for some years Germany was to be governed by a control commission but, despite its division into zones of occupation, it was to be treated as one unit; the question of its eastern boundaries was to be decided at a peace treaty. Events soon took an unexpected turn. The Allied Control Commission was unable to function for lack of unanimity and the entrusting of government authority into German hands came as early as 1949; but alas, there were two governments and a divided Germany. The peace treaty, on the other hand, is still as far off as ever. The reasons for this tragic division are that the European boundary between the two world power blocs runs right across Germany, and secondly, but at least equally important, that Germany is still widely distrusted for having started the war and for causing the death and suffering of millions of people.

The magnitude of destruction and loss of life suffered in the war were so tremendous that the human mind is scarcely able to comprehend it. The civilian casualties were unimaginable. Flattening of whole towns by bombing was started by Hitler in the invasion of Poland, but during the later stages of the war German cities suffered the same fate. Nevertheless, terrible as the loss of life due to air raids was, it represented only a relatively small proportion of the total. Much larger and even more invidious were the losses due to the ruthless suppression of any resistance against the Nazi terror and the application of the Nazi doctrine of the *Herrenvolk* (master race) pushed to its ultimate conclusion. Persecution of the Jews had begun immediately after Hitler's rise to power. Discriminatory laws and economic sanctions drove thousands from their homes to seek refuge in Britain and the United States. Soon increasing numbers of Jews together with other Germans considered to be "enemies of the state" were put into concentration camps; most never to return. During the war came the final abyss: the wholesale murder of Jews in towns of Poland and Russia or in the gas chambers of concentration camps. How many Jews lost their lives directly or indirectly through German action will never be known; according to estimates it was more than 6 million. It was, as Churchill said, "the greatest and most horrible crime ever committed in the whole history of the world". The mass murder of other peoples considered racially inferior was equally vast. The civilian losses of the Soviet Union (7 million people), Poland (over 4 million), and Yugoslavia (nearly 1½ million) were particularly high, but all countries that had come under German control experienced the Nazi terror. Once German control ceased the wrath of the people turned against the German population in their midst. The loss of as many as 3 million lives—again only estimates are possible—of the pre-war German population of East-central

and Eastern Europe apart from Russia, was also a tragedy of unimaginable magnitude. Against this background, merely to be expelled was a relatively kind fate.

The memories of these terrible events still cast a shadow over the relations between Germany and its neighbours, and not only those of the Soviet bloc. However, as new generations grow up, these wounds are beginning to heal. While the older generation has not yet come to terms with the past—the *unüberwundene Vergangenheit* as it is called—the young are able to look at it in a more detached light and, one must hope, will eventually re-establish a new basis for better mutual relations. West Germany, risen from the ruins to become one of the most prosperous countries in the world, has done much though possibly not yet enough to make amends, and the government of the economically much poorer G.D.R. has also acknowledged the German debt even if it has not made compensatory payments to individuals outside its borders. More important than any material amends is the existence of "a Germany which is ashamed of its past and has sworn it will never come back". These words were spoken in 1966 by the President of the Federal Parliament at the World Jewish Congress at Brussels, and the fact that a German was invited to address the assembly is a hopeful sign for the future.

Apart from coming to terms with the past, the other main German problem is the division of the country. It seems impossible to imagine that this division is final, but so far it has been hardening steadily. There are some rays of hope; the desire for reunification amongst the people on either side of the border is stronger than ever and even both governments, however contrary their proposals to achieve this reunification, profess that this is the long-term goal of their policies. Reunification will not come suddenly, but one must hope that some progress towards it will be made soon. It is a fallacy to believe that a division of Germany might be of value to world security. Countries divided against the wishes of their peoples cannot be so. There is the real danger that a continued division without prospects to end it will foster extremism and that this could be the spark to ignite the fuse wire—the barbed-wire cutting across Germany. If that were to happen it would not mean another Vietnam—terrible as that war is—but another world conflict.

The ruins of the Reichskanzlei (Chancellery) in Berlin where Hitler committed suicide in April 1945 are indicative of the state of the centres of most large German cities in May 1945. The Chancellery was shortly afterwards razed to the ground and there is now a public garden on the site where it stood but otherwise the rebuilding of the centre of Berlin (in the eastern part of the divided city) and of all other large towns is nearly completed.

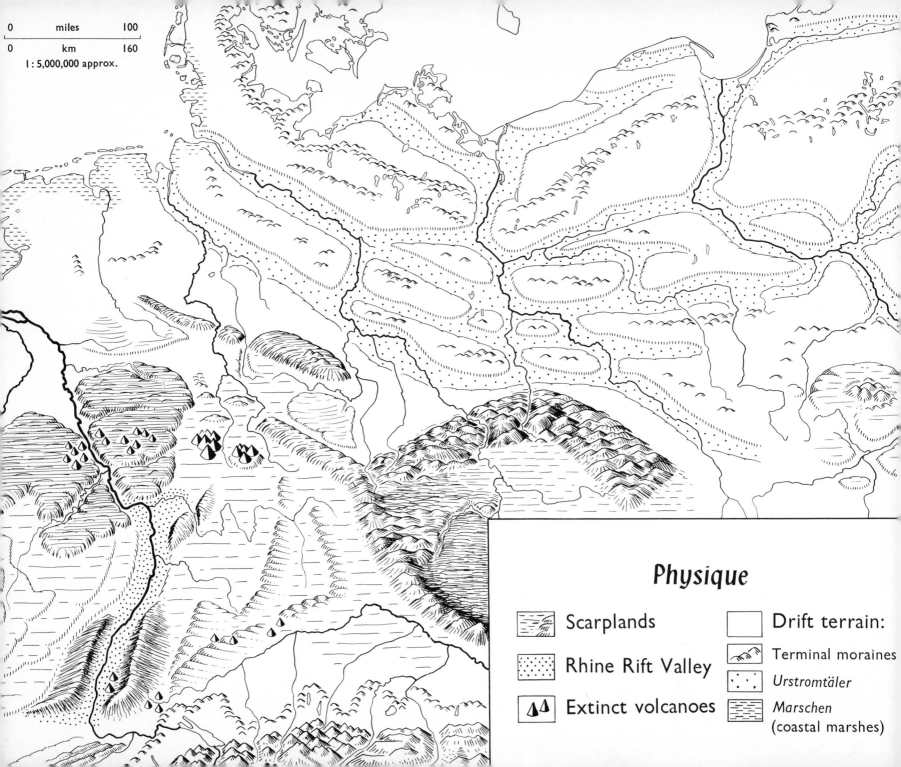

Physique

	Scarplands		Drift terrain:
	Rhine Rift Valley		Terminal moraines
			Urstromtäler
▲△	Extinct volcanoes		*Marschen* (coastal marshes)

0   miles   100

0   km   160

1 : 5,000,000 approx.

3. Physique

A glance at the map opposite shows that the surface of Germany is extremely diverse. Rocks from all epochs of the earth's history are found here and many different types of land-forms appear, from plains to rugged glacier-covered peaks. In spite of these diversities the surface forms show a clear trend in a west–easterly direction, and in an overall view Germany may be divided on the basis of these west–east land-forms into three major parts, the Uplands in the centre, the Alps in the south and the Lowland in the north.

The Uplands

The backbone of Germany is formed by the Uplands. These are mainly plateaux which rarely rise, however, above 1,000 metres. Generally speaking in their upper reaches they consist of gently undulating hills, but they frequently drop steeply to enclosed basins or river valleys. Because of their division into several groups the Uplands do not form a barrier between the north and south but leave a number of gaps through which the lines of communication pass without much difficulty.

Far back in the earth's history during the Palaeozoic Era, movements of the earth's crust caused dry land to rise, in what is now the Uplands, from a sea which stretched over the entire area of present-day Germany and beyond. In a tropical climate luxuriant

In some parts of the Uplands the younger covering rocks have been worn away and the ancient core of granite has become exposed. This is generally so in the highest parts—Black Forest, Bohemian Forest, Harz and Giant Mountains—but it occurs sometimes also at lower altitudes. In these cases granite is extensively quarried—as here in Silesia—to be used for paving-stones and in building.

In the Uplands the main valleys are often deeply incised into a gently rolling plateau surface, as is clearly shown in this view of the Rhine Gorge near the famous Lorelei. This is the result of the rivers deepening their beds while the *peneplains* (i.e. nearly level surfaces) to which the ancient Hercynian Mountains had been reduced rose to their present height during late Tertiary and Pleistocene times.

The Tertiary earth movements which shattered the worn-down Hercynian Mountains and began to raise them into the present Uplands were accompanied by much volcanic activity. The Siebengebirge—the seven mountains—at the northern entrance to the Rhine Gorge is one of the best-known examples of volcanic necks (i.e. the lava cores that remain after the mantle of ash has worn away). The Drachenfels (Dragon's Crag) in the centre of this picture is associated with the Siegfried legend and is visited annually by thousands of people.

Volcanic activity in the Uplands did not cease with the end of the Tertiary period but continued on a smaller scale until after the Ice Age. The most prominent resulting features are the Maare of the Eifel Mountains, circular lakes occupying the craters of gas explosions (left). Less striking in appearance are some fifty volcanic cones like the Mosenberg shown here (right), and deposits of volcanic ash which occur in considerable thickness north of Koblenz where they are quarried and made into excellent artificial building stone.

swamp forests developed along the shores; some of these forests were later buried beneath more recent deposits and turned into coal. Thus the coalfields of the Saar, Aachen, the Ruhr, Saxony and Silesia adjoin the Uplands. The Hercynian Mountains, as these most ancient of the German mountains have been termed, became worn down and parts were once again covered by the sea; thus they became covered by the deposits which accumulated at the sea bottom. Uplift of the land above the waves and re-advances of the sea alternated a number of times during the next epoch, the Mesozoic Era.

During the Tertiary Era that followed, the earth movements became particularly pronounced. This was the time when the young folded mountains of the earth arose and this "Alpine storm" had its repercussions on the area which was to become the Uplands. There, together with a general uplifting of the land, which thus became mountainous once more, a fracturing of the surface took place; large sections tilted, others collapsed, whilst neighbouring parts were lifted higher. The Rhine Valley between Basle and Wiesbaden is a section which was faulted down; a valley of this kind is called a rift valley or *Graben*. In contrast to that a piece of land thrust up is called a block mountain or *Horst*; an example of the latter is the Thuringian Forest.

Beneath the solid earth's crust there is a zone where the rocks are in a plastic or liquid state owing to the very much higher temperature prevailing in the earth's interior. When the surface was fractured during the Tertiary storm this fiery liquid came in some places very near to the surface, while in others it reached the surface itself and gave rise to volcanic eruptions. As a result of these events in the Uplands there are now, in addition to the hills formed of sedimentary rocks, volcanic mountains consisting of various types of igneous rock (e.g. the Vogelsberg, lying at the northern end of the Rhine Rift Valley).

In some of the low-lying areas around and within the Uplands, there occurred during the Tertiary Era other periods when luxuriant forests became covered by later deposits and the product of this submergence was brown coal, in which Germany is rich. (The major brown coalfields are west of Cologne, around Leipzig and in Lower Lusatia.)

The severe climate of the Ice Age shattered the rocks of the Upland plateaux and the large blocks that remained after removal of the smaller fragments form "block fields" or on slopes "block streams". These are best developed in the Bunter sandstone of the Odenwald, shown here, and were used there as a ready quarry by the Romans—as this giant pillar illustrates.

The last period of the earth's history, which includes the geological present, is called the Quaternary Era. The characteristic event during its first phase, the Pleistocene, was a deterioration of the climate, which gave rise to the formation of glaciers in Scandinavia and the Alps. From there they pushed into Middle Europe, which in the north and in the south became covered by ice-sheets. The ice melted away and advanced, alternately, at least five times until, about 10,000 to 12,000 years ago, the climate became approximately what it is today. The Uplands were too low to develop an ice-sheet of their own. A few tiny glaciers appeared on the higher parts, the Black Forest, the Bohemian Forest and the Giant Mountains, but on the whole the Uplands were an ice-free corridor between the northern and southern ice-sheets; nevertheless they looked very different from today. It was much colder and the Uplands were covered by a meagre tundra vegetation instead of forest. The ground was frozen down to a considerable depth and only the uppermost part thawed during the brief summers. Frost action shattered the exposed rocks and soil creep flattened the slopes, especially those facing south and west where the sun had more effect. In sheltered basins the north winds deposited a fine dust which they had picked up in the completely barren stretches in front of the ice-sheet. This is the valuable loess, the basis of the very fertile soils which support the intensive agriculture of the northern fringe of the Uplands, the *Börde* zone, and of some parts of the Upland zone itself.

During the Ice Age, local glaciers formed on the highest parts of the Uplands, where they have left features reminiscent of the Alps, like this cirque lake, the Feldbergsee, in the Black Forest.

The Alps

We have already mentioned the "Alpine storm" which was responsible for the present height of the Uplands. The greatest effect, however, of this gigantic upheaval was the formation of the second of the major physical regions of Germany, the Alps. The ancient Hercynian Mountains had originally extended to the south of the present Uplands. Very soon (in geological terms) after their formation, this southern portion sank and became covered by a vast sea on whose bed thick layers of deposits accumulated. When once again a mountain system began to rise in this area, almost all trace of the former Hercynian Mountains had been obliterated. This happened towards the end of the Mesozoic Era. Still within the same geological period (the Cretaceous), these later mountains were worn down and submerged and only negligible features of these earliest Alps are preserved in the Alps as they are today. The present Alps date from the later Tertiary epoch, but they continued to rise right into the Quaternary Era. Even before climatic deterioration set in, however, the appearance of the Alps had been greatly altered by "sub-aerial" erosion—by weather and water; now they were covered by a mantle of ice. Many features of the Alps are the result of the erosive powers of the glaciers. High up there are the cirques, hollows where the ice accumulated before gradually moving down; there are steep-sided trough-shaped valleys, widened by the glaciers from their formerly much narrower V shape. The glaciers which, unlike water, were able to move upwards as well as downwards, excavated basins which are now often occupied by lakes. Only a small section of the Alps comes within the boundaries of Germany but all these features are found there.

The effect of the Alpine glaciers was not confined to the Alps themselves. At least five times the glaciers pushed into the Alpine Foreland and the lines to which they reached are marked by the crescents of terminal moraines, ranges of hills formed by the rubble which the glaciers took with them on their way. After the glaciers

Of all the features which date back to the Ice Age, none is more attractive than the many lakes which now fill cirques, overdeepened valley troughs and U-shaped valleys where the glaciers once stretched their huge lobes of ice into the foothill zone. This is a cirque lake in the **Allgäu Alps**.

Gravel-sheets like this one on the anastomosing (braided) Isar river (at its confluence with the Danube) were formed during the Ice Age by every Alpine river after it had left behind the zone of foothills and terminal moraines. The main difference between the gravel-sheets still being formed and those of the Pleistocene period is that the latter are incomparably larger and form an almost continuous zone south of the Danube.

had melted away lakes formed behind many of these moraines and although some have since become overgrown and turned into peat bogs, the great number of beautiful lakes is still a characteristic feature of the Alpine Foreland. The indirect effects of the Pleistocene Alpine glaciers extend even further. The melt-waters carried pebbles and sand with them and formed extensive terraces and gravel-sheets on their way to the Danube. Unless they are covered by loess, which was also laid down here (as in the *Börde*), they form poor soils and support only extensive pine forests. This applies to all the glacio-fluvial deposits (glacial material laid down by rivers) of the last glacial period as these are contemporary with or later than the deposition of loess.

The Lowland

The North German Lowland resembles the Alpine Foreland in owing most of its features to the Pleistocene glaciers; it is therefore very similar to the latter, though everything is on a vastly larger scale. The solid rocks appear on the surface in so very few places that the Northern Lowland can justly be called a child of the Ice Age. Here it was the Scandinavian glaciers which did the work of transformation and at their greatest extent they stretched right to the edge of the Uplands. The moraines of the earlier glaciations (they form, for instance, the well-known Lüneburg Heath) are not very striking since they were flattened by soil creep during later glacial periods, but the moraines of the last glaciation are well preserved and form hills of 100 to 300 metres. Since the edge of the ice-sheet did not always run along the same line there are a number of concentric crescents of these moraines corresponding to different glacial periods and advances of the ice-sheet. Parallel to these run the *Urstromtäler*, shallow, very broad valleys which were excavated by the melt-waters from the ice-sheet on their way to the North Sea. The greatest variety of landscape is found in those areas of the Northern Lowland which the ice abandoned last. Parts of the ice became buried under outwash material—the pebbles and sand dumped by the melt-water—and when these masses of ice eventually melted, the ground subsided and the numerous kettle-hole lakes were formed. Blockage of the drainage by moraines also resulted in the formation of lakes, and though

Germany cannot compete with Finland as the "land of the thousand lakes" there is a very great number of them, large and small, stretching from eastern Schleswig-Holstein and Mecklenburg to southern East Prussia.

The latest events of geological history on German soil—the last advances and the final melting away of the giant ice-sheets, the last volcanic eruptions in the Eifel Mountains and the retreat of the North Sea coast from a line much farther north to somewhere near its present position—were witnessed by early man. These earliest peoples, small in number, lived by hunting, fishing and gathering edible plants. In their effect on the landscape they barely differed from the beasts, so that the landscape at that time was entirely the result of physical forces. This is called the *Urlandschaft* or primeval landscape. The change, and at the same time the beginning of human geography, comes with the Late Stone Age (Neolithic Period) when man, with his primitive agriculture and his flocks of domestic animals, began to alter the face of the German landscape until it came to look as it does today.

Apart from the High Alps there are hardly any true natural landscapes left in Germany today. There are, of course, numerous remarkable natural features—"monuments of nature"—and a good many areas whose landscapes, not yet affected by technology, give at least the illusion of being natural. In an industrial society, areas like these are of great value as a source of recuperation for mind and body. For some time many natural features have been protected by law, and small areas have been set aside as preserves for field study. However, with one exception, a part of the Lüneburg Heath which was acquired by a private organisation in 1909 to protect it from being spoiled, the protection of larger areas as "nature parks" is a very recent phenomenon. Since 1957, twenty-five areas varying in size between about 40 square kilometres (the Siebengebirge) and nearly 1,500 square kilometres (the Palatinate Forest) have been assigned for preservation in West Germany. The "nature parks" at present constitute about 5 per cent of the area of the country, but there are proposals to increase their number to cover a total area of 10 per cent.

North-west of Königsberg (Kaliningrad) lies the Samland peninsula. On some stretches there the waves have undercut the boulder clay and given rise to a line of cliffs.

A particularly attractive inheritance of the Ice Age in the Northern Lowland are the many lakes of Mecklenburg, Pomerania and East Prussia. Here is a view of lake Müritz in Mecklenburg, the largest of all the lakes that lie completely within Germany.

29

4. Climate

The weather is a major topic of conversation in Britain and also in Germany—which shows how changeable it is. Generally speaking, Germany's climate is similar to that of Britain, and not only on account of its changeability. Both countries are situated in the temperate zone where the weather is largely dictated by the prevailing westerly winds, and in neither case are there any high mountains running north–south to prevent the westerlies from penetrating into the hinterland. But though similar, the climate of Germany is by no means identical to that of Britain. One reason for the difference is that Germany lies nearer the centre of the Continent and its climate is therefore more "continental"; this means that the contrast between the summer and winter temperatures is greater, that the winters are colder and last longer, and that thunderstorms with heavy showers or hail are more frequent. Since these occur mainly during the height of the summer, the month with the highest rainfall over most of Germany is July instead of October to December as in most parts of Britain, which has a "maritime" climate. This is, however, a very general characterisation.

It is in the west–east rather than the north–south direction that variations occur; and relief is another very potent factor.

The two principal and most easily appreciable climatic elements are temperature and rainfall (this term includes all types of precipitation). Let us look at these separately.

The Pattern of Temperatures

Since the sun is the ultimate source of almost all heat on the earth's surface, we would expect temperature to increase as one goes southward. The maps of the actual mean temperatures for different months, however, show that this is not true of Germany. If we ignore the Rhine Rift Valley, which is a special case, the summer temperatures of South Germany are no higher than those of North Germany and, with the exception of the very north-east the winter is even colder in the south than in the north. Even more clearly brought out by the map is the fact that there is also a decrease in average winter temperature from west to east, which again does not

agree with the general rule that latitude governs temperature.

Looking more closely at the pattern formed by the isotherms (the lines connecting all points with the same temperature) we can make the following observations:

During the summer months a wedge-shaped area of high temperatures, situated between the Baltic Heights and the Central Uplands, stretches from Poland into Germany and reaches as far as the Saale river south of Magdeburg; a second area of high temperatures is found along the Rhine from Basle to Bonn; it also extends into the main tributary valleys, the Moselle, Main and Neckar, and has an exclave along the shores of Lake Constance. The areas with the lowest temperatures are the major groups of the Uplands and Germany's part of the Alps and their foothills.

During the winter the temperatures are not merely lower than those of the summer but the distribution pattern of the relatively warm and cold areas is very different. True, the Rhine Valley still ranks amongst the warmest areas; it is, however, no longer isolated but is joined to the much larger area in the north-west. In these regions

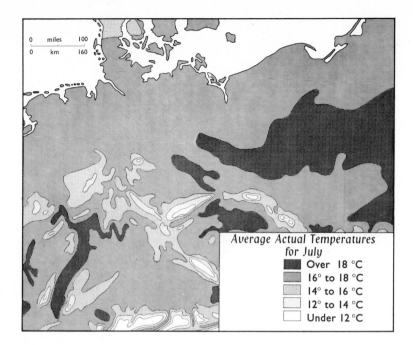

Average Actual Temperatures
for July
Over 18 °C
16° to 18 °C
14° to 16 °C
12° to 14 °C
Under 12 °C

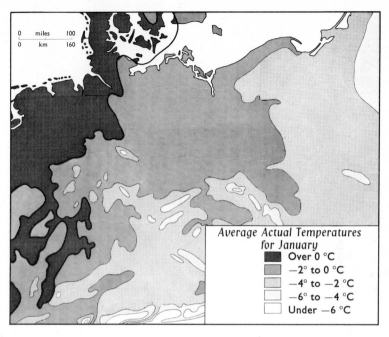

Average Actual Temperatures
for January
Over 0 °C
−2° to 0 °C
−4° to −2 °C
−6° to −4 °C
Under −6 °C

the mean temperatures of even the coldest month, January, are above freezing, although days do occur with temperatures below 0 °C or when it freezes from midnight to midnight. But compared with the rest of Germany their number is small. Cologne and the area west of it, which are particularly favoured in this respect, experience in an average year less than sixty days when temperatures fall below freezing-point, and a mere ten days or so of twenty-four hours' unbroken frost.

The areas with the lowest winter temperatures likewise coincide only partially with the summer pattern. The Uplands and the Alps again stand out as being particularly cold, but in the first place the colder areas have, south of the Main river, become considerably more extensive and joined to each other, and secondly they have found a counterpart in eastern East Prussia. There the temperature falls below freezing for over 140 days, and for about 60 days it stays below freezing all day.

What, then, are the causes which override the normal tendency for temperature to increase southwards, and which give rise to the conditions described above? They are principally two: altitude, and the increasing distance from the moderating influence of the North Sea and the Atlantic.

The absence of a temperature rise southward can in the first instance be explained by the general rise of the land to the south. That this is so becomes clearer when we look at a map which shows the temperatures recalculated to their values at sea-level so that the effect of altitude is eliminated: on such a map the isotherms of the mean annual temperatures do run roughly in a west–easterly direction. The pattern of the sea-level isotherms for July is very similar and again shows this temperature increase southwards.

On the other hand the sea-level isotherms for January temperatures run almost due north to south and seem to disregard completely the effect of latitude. This shows that during the cold season the moderating influence exerted by the Atlantic and the North Sea becomes particularly great. The sea retains the heat received during the summer and by means of the westerly winds extends its influence eastwards. On the other hand, the great land-mass of the European continent to the east of Germany becomes very cold and acts as a source of cold air moving west. Germany, more than any other country in Europe, is the battleground between the mild maritime and the cold continental air masses. The fortunes of the battle vary greatly: at one time extreme cold may grip the whole of Middle Europe and extend well into Western Europe, while at other periods mild maritime air may advance as far as Russia. The fact remains that owing to the short winter days the role of latitude (i.e. the length of day) is negligible, and consequently we find this general temperature gradient from west to east.

Western and eastern air masses still conflict during the summer, but with roles reversed. It is now the west which acts as a source of cool air whereas the interior of the Continent becomes rather warm. The absolute difference in temperature between maritime and continental air is now less, too, so that latitude becomes the overriding factor. This results in a temperature gradient from north to south, which is, however, as we have noted, disguised by the relief.

Spring comes earliest in Germany to the Rhine valley between Basle and Cologne and its main tributaries, the lower Main, Neckar and Moselle (shown here). These regions enjoy the most favourable climate as their vineyards, orchards, and tobacco and maize fields clearly indicate.

Meteorological instruments cannot indicate as satisfactorily as plants the combined effects of all climatic elements, firstly by the very presence of certain species in areas where they find a congenial climate, and secondly by their growth responses to climatic conditions in every month of the year. In certain parts of the tropics, where these conditions are nearly uniform, there is little variation from month to month, but in the central latitudes of the temperate zone within which Germany is situated, they are particularly pronounced. They vary not only with altitude but also regionally and locally. Generally we speak of the four seasons and relate the different appearance of the plant cover to them; these seasons of the calendar, however, take into account only one climatic factor, insolation, and are therefore no more than a rough guide. As everyone knows from experience, the aspect of the landscape we associate with spring does not appear overnight on 21 March, but comes gradually; the more southerly, lower and otherwise climatically favoured regions being the first, and the more northerly, higher and otherwise handicapped parts being the last to experience spring conditions.

Over the past fifty years a branch of climatology, called phenology, which studies this changing appearance of the plant cover, has been greatly developed and has contributed considerably towards a better understanding of the climate of Germany.

The main stages of the vegetation cycles were observed in numerous places over many years, the average dates of the occurrence of these phenological landmarks were calculated and many maps were drawn showing the onset and duration of the various actual seasons which they characterise. Combined, these maps show the lengths of the growing season for the different parts of Germany, and the differing speed at which the actual seasons follow each other. The two maps reproduced here show at what dates different areas experience conditions characteristic of the middle of spring and the height of summer and together span the length of the major growing season. On the map "Onset of Apple Blossom", the Rhine Valley above Düsseldorf and its major tributary valleys emerge as the most favoured climatically, followed by the rest of the low-lying parts of the extreme west of Germany and a few similar outlying regions along the Saale and upper Elbe valleys and the Danube below Ratisbon. The last areas to experience spring are the Alps and Upland heights and the north-east. The map "Beginning of Rye Harvest" reveals a greatly changed pattern of climatic conditions at the height of the summer. Although the Rhine Valley and its tributaries are again amongst the regions which are the earliest to experience these conditions, they no longer constitute the largest area. This has shifted to the most continental parts of Germany, the northernmost part of the Alpine Foreland and the southern part of the Northern Lowland east of the Harz Mountains. The most retarded areas are also different. The effect of altitude is now even more pronounced and the coastal regions of the North Sea are amongst those where summer comes relatively late.

As the year progresses, the time lag between "early" and "late" regions decreases and late autumn, phenologically characterised by the turning of the leaves of deciduous broadleaf trees, sets in towards the middle of October almost uniformly throughout Germany. The only distinction then between the more and less favoured areas is the length of this season which continues in the Rhine Valley after winter has overtaken the Alps and Upland heights and the plants have become covered by snow.

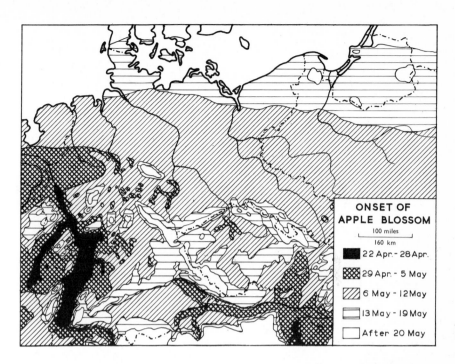

ONSET OF
APPLE BLOSSOM

100 miles
160 km

22 Apr. - 28 Apr.
29 Apr. - 5 May
6 May - 12 May
13 May - 19 May
After 20 May

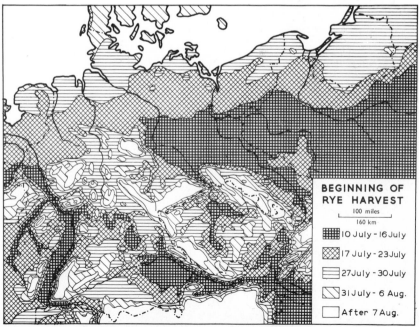

BEGINNING OF
RYE HARVEST

100 miles
160 km

10 July - 16 July
17 July - 23 July
27 July - 30 July
31 July - 6 Aug.
After 7 Aug.

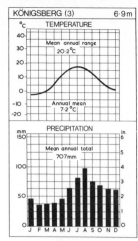

EMDEN (1) 7·8 m

TEMPERATURE
Mean annual range 15·5°C
Annual mean 8·5°C

PRECIPITATION
Mean annual total 736mm

J F M A M J J A S O N D

LÜBECK (2) 8·7 m

TEMPERATURE
Mean annual range 16·9°C
Annual mean 8·1°C

PRECIPITATION
Mean annual total 632mm

J F M A M J J A S O N D

KÖNIGSBERG (3) 6·9 m

TEMPERATURE
Mean annual range 20·2°C
Annual mean 7·2°C

PRECIPITATION
Mean annual total 707mm

J F M A M J J A S O N D

TILSIT (4) 17·7m

TEMPERATURE
Mean annual range 21·1°C
Annual mean 6·6°C

PRECIPITATION
Mean annual total 728mm

J F M A M J J A S O N D

COLOGNE (5) 55·5m

TEMPERATURE
Mean annual range 16·0°C
Annual mean 10·2°C

PRECIPITATATION
Mean annual total 696mm

J F M A M J J A S O N D

BERLIN (6) 56·4m

TEMPERATURE
Mean annual range 18·6°C
Annual mean 8·4°C

PRECIPITATION
Mean annual total 587mm

J F M A M J J A S O N D

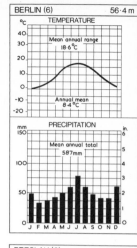

HEIDELBERG (7) 117·0m

TEMPERATURE
Mean annual range 17·6°C
Annual mean 10·2°C

PRECIPITATION
Mean annual total 718mm

J F M A M J J A S O N D

BRESLAU (8) 145·5 m

TEMPERATURE
Mean annual range 19·9°C
Annual mean 8·7°C

PRECIPITATION
Mean annual total 592mm

J F M A M J J A S O N D

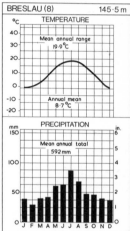

MUNICH (9) 523·8m

TEMPERATURE
Mean annual range 19·3°C
Annual mean 7·4°C

PRECIPITATION
Mean annual total 935mm

J F M A M J J A S O N D

ZUGSPITZE (10) 2986·2m

TEMPERATURE
Mean annual range 13·0°C
Annual mean −5·0°C

PRECIPITATION
Mean annual total 2390mm

J F M A M J J A S O N D

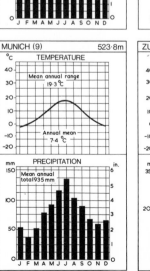

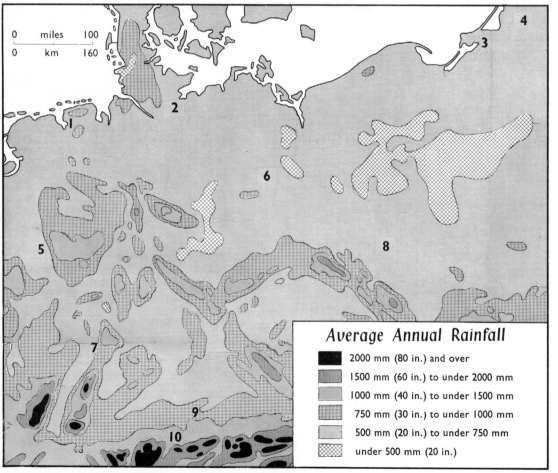

0 miles 100
0 km 160

Average Annual Rainfall

■ 2000 mm (80 in.) and over

1500 mm (60 in.) to under 2000 mm

1000 mm (40 in.) to under 1500 mm

750 mm (30 in.) to under 1000 mm

500 mm (20 in.) to under 750 mm

under 500 mm (20 in.)

34

The Pattern of Rainfall

The second principal climatic element is precipitation. Lying as it does in the westerly wind belt, Germany receives most of its precipitation at all seasons from the low-pressure systems known as cyclones or depressions, which abound in these latitudes. The reason for the summer maximum is that in this season a relatively stationary system of high pressure (an anti-cyclone) lies over the eastern Atlantic while low pressure prevails over the Continent, thus causing maritime air to flow eastwards. In winter an almost stationary anti-cyclone lies over northern Europe and low pressure prevails over the Atlantic, thus giving rise to easterly air streams which at times prevent humid maritime air from penetrating into Germany.

Looking at the map opposite we see that Germany has neither an excess nor a dearth of precipitation. This map also shows the influence of relief and of the eastern land-masses. The Uplands and the Alps stand out as the areas of highest precipitation, and the rise of the land southward is paralleled by an increase in precipitation. Sheltered valleys and basins like the northern part of the Rhine Rift Valley, the northern Oder Valley and the eastern Harz Foreland are clearly identified by low precipitation of less than 500 millimetres.

The isohyets (the lines linking all points with the same rainfall) show a decrease of precipitation eastwards too, a further indication of the increasing continentality of the climate towards the east. This is further emphasised by an increase in the frequency of thunderstorms in this direction and also southwards. Heligoland experiences on an annual average 12 days with thunderstorms, while Königsberg (Kaliningrad) in East Prussia has 21, Grünberg (Zielona Gora) in Silesia 27 and Munich 32 days.

The Climate of the Mountains

We have already referred a number of times to the modification of climate by relief. Mountains, indeed, almost "make their own climate".

It is generally true that the higher the mountains the higher the rainfall (or snowfall), the lower the temperature and the longer the cold season. But there are finer points to consider. Because of the direction of the rain-bearing winds a mountain situated in the west experiences a considerably higher precipitation than a mountain of the same height farther east. The western outposts of the German Uplands even experience a "maritime" rainfall maximum in December like Devon and Cornwall, the Pennines and most of Scotland, instead of in July like the surrounding German countryside.

The climatic snow line, i.e. the contour line above which more snow falls than melts during the year, lies in the German Alps at about 2,700 metres, but because of the ruggedness of the limestone mountains which lack gentler slopes above this altitude, the snow does not find much of a foothold. There are thus only very few and very small glaciers. One of them lies in the cirque between the two main peaks of the Watzmann, which gives the small town of Berchtesgaden its unique background.

One of the most spectacular features of a mountain climate is the formation of a low cloud layer as the downflow of cold air during the night gives rise to a temperature inversion (a reversal of the normal decrease of temperature with increasing altitude). Only the peaks rise like islands above this sea of clouds.

Mountain regions are also different from the plains in that their climate varies over very short distances. There are not only the differences between their western and eastern flanks and the peaks and the valleys, but even between the two sides of the same valley where, because of its inclination, the south-facing slope receives the sun's rays vertically and thus enjoys for a time practically tropical sunshine. If the geological conditions are the same on either side this climatic factor is clearly reflected in the land-use. Whereas dark woods reach nearly to the valley bottom on the north-facing slope (the *ubac*), on the south-facing slope (the *adret*) the forests have been cleared and farmhouses surrounded by fields and meadows stretch up to great heights. The reason for this is not only the favourable sunshine during the summer but also the sunshine these slopes enjoy during the winter and spring, resulting in an early melting of the snow and thus a lengthening of the growing season.

In the Alps the importance of sunshine in speeding the melting of the snow is rivalled by that of a particular wind, the *Föhn*. This is a warm and very dry south wind which has earned the nickname "snow-eater". It starts quite suddenly and when it occurs in winter the temperature rises within a few hours from well below freezing to well above. The snow shrinks as one watches it and on steep slopes it becomes so heavy and slippery that it loses its hold and thunders down as an avalanche.

(Avalanches do, however, occur also for a number of other reasons.)

Changes of Weather

In an area where frequent change in the weather is a typical feature of the climate we must also add a few words about the sequence of the weather conditions during the year. This sequence is not completely haphazard, as might appear, for there is a discernible pattern.

During the winter clear skies, low-lying haze and low temperatures are typical for mid-December, mid-January and early February, while a thaw at Christmas is a very regular occurrence. In spring only the latter part of March and the last week of May offer a good chance of steady fine weather. Otherwise there are typical April conditions—rapid alternation between sunny "high-pressure" weather and relapses of cold weather with showers of snow or sleet and gusty winds. The summer weather is more or less unpredictable. Rain tends to be particularly frequent in the middle of June, the end of July and the beginning of August, but this does not mean that rain is unlikely at other times; one can only say that there is a better chance of fine weather at the end of June, the middle of July and the end of August. The autumn is very much more reliable for holidays, with regular fine periods in early and late September and again at the end of October.

When weather conditions are favourable there is a unique view from the Zugspitze (2,964 m), Germany's highest point, over the peaks of the Austrian Alps. The double cloud layer and in particular the high cirrostratus cloud front indicate the onset of the Föhn which will soon be followed by prolonged rain.

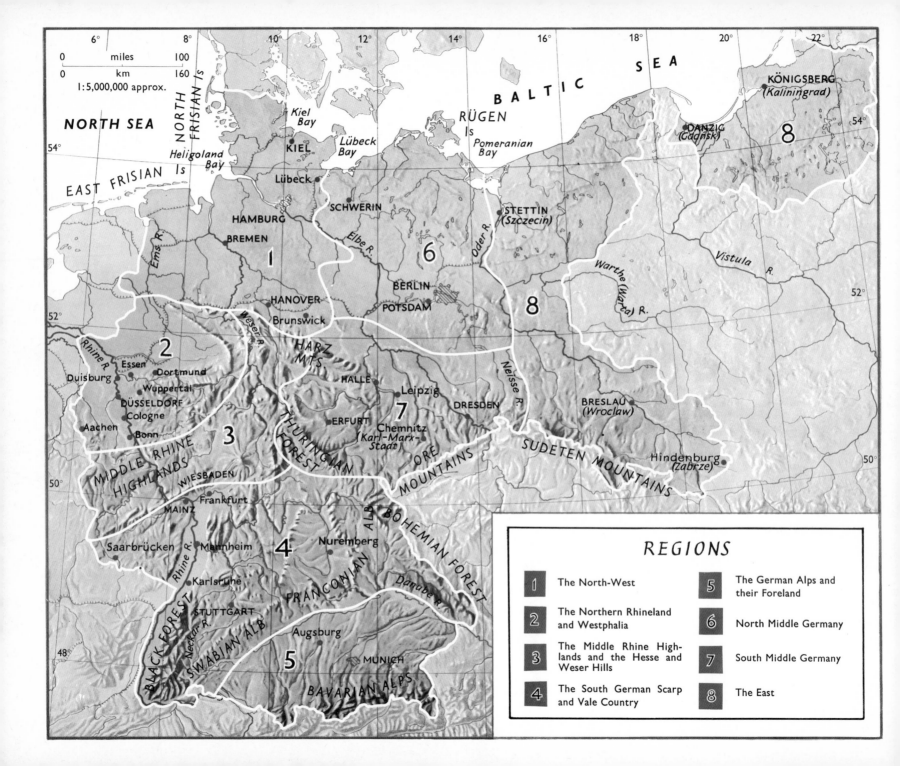

REGIONS

1	The North-West
2	The Northern Rhineland and Westphalia
3	The Middle Rhine Highlands and the Hesse and Weser Hills
4	The South German Scarp and Vale Country
5	The German Alps and their Foreland
6	North Middle Germany
7	South Middle Germany
8	The East

NORTH SEA

BALTIC SEA

NORTH FRISIAN Is

EAST FRISIAN Is

Heligoland Bay

Kiel Bay

Lübeck Bay

Pomeranian Bay

RÜGEN Is

KÖNIGSBERG (Kaliningrad)

DANZIG (Gdansk)

KIEL

Lübeck

SCHWERIN

STETTIN (Szczecin)

HAMBURG

BREMEN

Ems R.

HANOVER

Brunswick

BERLIN

POTSDAM

Elbe R.

Oder R.

Warthe (Warta) R.

Vistula R.

HARZ MTS.

Weser R.

Rhine R.

Essen

Duisburg

Dortmund

Wuppertal

DÜSSELDORF

Cologne

Aachen

Bonn

MIDDLE RHINE HIGHLANDS

HALLE

Leipzig

DRESDEN

ERFURT

Chemnitz (Karl-Marx-Stadt)

THURINGIAN FOREST

Neisse R.

ORE MOUNTAINS

SUDETEN MOUNTAINS

BRESLAU (Wroclaw)

Hindenburg (Zabrze)

WIESBADEN

Frankfurt

MAINZ

Saarbrücken

Mannheim

Rhine R.

Nuremberg

ALB

BOHEMIAN FOREST

Karlsruhe

BLACK FOREST

STUTTGART

Neckar R.

SWABIAN ALB

FRANCONIAN

Danube R.

Augsburg

MUNICH

BAVARIAN ALPS

miles 0 100

km 0 160

1:5,000,000 approx.

PART TWO

The Regions

Rarely is a country small and uniform enough for an overall view to bring home its geographical personality. In order to understand a country, the geographer has to describe and study its constituent units or "regions". What, then, are the regions of Germany? No simple answer is possible and almost as many regional subdivisions have been suggested as there are books on the geography of Germany. While this clearly shows that there is not one indisputable regional pattern, there are nevertheless certain basic facts which must not be ignored if the chosen pattern is to have validity —for instance, the role of the North Sea coast, the important influence of the Ruhr industry or, much more recently, the existence of two political boundaries: the "Oder-Neisse line" and the "Iron Curtain". Political boundaries within a country are normally of little geographical significance: in this case, however, they separate from each other parts of Germany which are distinct geographically because changes in the landscape have arisen as a result of the differing economies and use of resources. The large-scale population change in the East, from German to Slav, is yet another of the factors which accounts for differences in the geography of West Germany, Middle Germany, and the lands east of the Oder and Neisse.

Pottenstein in Franconia: a small town in the South German Scarp and Vale Country.

5. The North-West

Politically this region consists of four Länder (provinces with a good deal of "home rule" like Northern Ireland): Schleswig-Holstein, most of Lower Saxony, and the Hanseatic cities of Bremen and Hamburg, whose boundaries enclose considerably more territory than their built-up area, and whose city senates have the status of a Land government. Part of Bremen's territory, the outpost of Bremerhaven, is an exclave.

Major cities (in thousands) arranged according to number of inhabitants in 1939:

	1939	1968
Hamburg	1711·9	1826·4
Hanover (Hannover)	471·0	524·5
Bremen	424·1	602·1
Kiel	273·7	268·9
Brunswick (Braunschweig)	196·1	227·3
Lübeck	154·8	242·4
Bremerhaven	138·7	148·5
Wilhelmshaven	113·7	102·3
Oldenburg	79·0	130·7
Hildesheim	72·1	97·1
Flensburg	70·9	96·1
Salzgitter	—	117·0
Wolfsburg	—	84·7

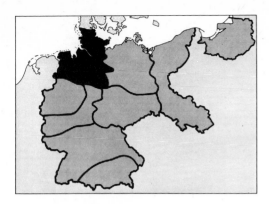

There are few natural features on the map which look as clear and as definite as the coastline. But nothing could be more misleading than to think of the German North Sea coast in such terms. Every year the coastline changes to some extent; and vastly greater changes occurred during historic and prehistoric times. At about the time of the birth of Christ the situation along the German North Sea coast was such that the sea had built up a zone of marshy land, or *Marschen*, in front of the boulder clay hills, and people ventured out on to it. Little did they realise that this land, which seemed a free gift from the sea, would have to be defended against it in one of the fiercest struggles ever waged by mankind against nature, and that it would have to be paid for in future centuries by thousands of lives.

The North Sea—a Liability and an Asset

At first all appeared safe enough. Only very rarely was a storm tide so high as to cause concern. When this began to happen more frequently, people built mounds and placed their homesteads on top of them; when later they found that these mounds were no longer sufficiently high, they gradually raised them higher still. As long as only the winter storm tides flooded the land, the crops of hay and summer grain were safe, but from about A.D. 800 onwards, even summer tides occasionally rose high enough to flood the land.

Now the inhabitants had to decide whether to give up the struggle or to protect not only their homesteads but their farmland as well. They chose the latter course. To prevent further flooding they built dams of clay to enclose a number of settlement mounds and an area of land (a polder or *Koog*). Later, dams were built which linked these polders with the higher hinterland and with each other. It was thus that the construction of dykes began, but the worst part of the struggle was still to come and it was not for some centuries that people became sufficiently experienced in constructing dykes for them to afford real safety. At first the dykes would hold for a while, but then some winter's storm tide would flood over and breach them, causing more loss of life than if there had been no dykes. Old chronicles tell the story of these great catastrophes when sometimes within a few hours thousands of hectares were flooded and many villages wiped out. Before A.D. 1000 the present bays were all well cultivated and densely settled land, and the North Frisian Islands along the coast of Schleswig-Holstein were then either part of the mainland or at least considerably larger than today. The last great flood was on the night of All Saints' Day in 1570; so many dykes broke that the whole coast from Holland to northern Jutland was flooded, and uncounted thousands of people were drowned. Little wonder, then, that the people of the coastal lowland called the North Sea the "Murder Sea". But they did not give up; they rebuilt the dykes and made them so high and strong that later storm tides were unable to cause damage in any way comparable with that which had occurred before 1600.

What is more, after being on the defensive for some 1,500 years, man went over to the offensive. Polder after polder was reclaimed from the mudbanks. During the present century alone about 12,000 hectares of fertile land have so far been reclaimed. This coastal zone of marine silt is extremely fertile, and ranks amongst the best farmland in Germany. Here are to be found the largest farmhouses and the richest farms. The polders which were dyked during earlier periods are devoted to animal husbandry, dairy farming and fattening of cattle; the more recently reclaimed polders produce excellent crops of wheat and roots. Influenced by the large market which Hamburg affords, those along the lower course of the Elbe have come to specialise in market-gardening and fruit-growing. The constant threat of the sea was nearly forgotten. But yet again the "Murder Sea" proved itself true to its name. In the early hours of 17 February 1962 onshore gales resulted in the highest tide ever recorded and in numerous breaches of dykes. As no flood warning had been given, it caught people in their sleep. In Hamburg alone, 312 casualties was the tragic toll.

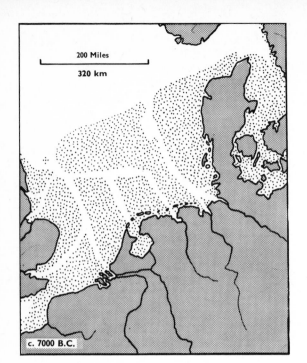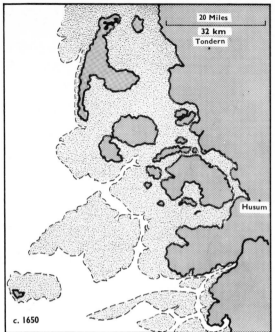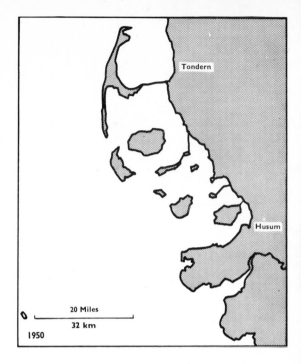

CHANGES IN THE COASTLINE

The faintly stippled areas in the first map show the probable extent of the land during the Middle Stone Age. In the second map the stippled areas show the probable extent in the thirteenth century.

So far we have looked at the sea as a dangerous enemy, but the benefits which Germany has derived and still derives from its coasts are far greater than the damage it inflicts. It gives Germany a share in the rich fishing grounds of the North Sea and the North Atlantic. The German fishing fleet, the most modern in the world because it had to be built up again from practically nothing after 1945, is third in size (after Great Britain and Norway) among the European countries. The possession of this coast has also enabled Germany to establish direct trade connections with all the sea-going countries of the world. Although, unlike Britain, not an island, Germany has a long tradition of seafaring. During the late Middle Ages, the *Hanse*, a powerful league of ports and cities, had the trade monopoly all round the Baltic and extended its influence to the North Sea ports, many of which—amongst them London—granted trade privileges. After the discovery of America and the

sea routes to the Far East the Baltic became a backwater and even the major German North Sea ports of Bremen, Emden and Hamburg were unable to retain their former importance. The advent of the German Empire in 1871 enabled the natural advantages once again to be used to the full, and the main ports quickly began to grow. Before the outbreak of the First World War in 1914 Germany had a merchant navy of 3 million gross tons, second only to Britain's, and Hamburg competed with Antwerp for the lead amongst the ports on the European continent.

The First World War and its aftermath were a terrible set-back to German seafaring. But with the same determination that they had used against the sea in defence of their land, the Germans set out to rebuild the merchant fleet and recapture lost trade. Hamburg's population passed the 1 million mark in 1925, and by 1939 the merchant navy had grown to 4 million gross tons. The

The small island of Heligoland, which has been part of the German Reich since 1890, is the farthest from the German mainland, but for this very reason it is of great importance to shipping. Its lighthouse is a valuable landmark and its harbour gives welcome shelter to small craft in heavy seas. The Heligoland life-boat has rescued many people. During both world wars it was a German submarine base and the blasting of the submarine shelters after the Second War nearly wrecked the island. Harbour and housing have been rebuilt since it was handed back to Germany in 1953 and once more it attracts many tourists. Being out-side the German customs boundaries it offers an additional attraction compared to other resorts—duty-free drinks and tobacco.

Wind and weather have given character to the face of this Heligo-land seaman. It was people like this who waged the centuries-old struggle against the sea.

Second World War was incomparably more damaging than the First to German ports and shipping. The ports suffered terribly from bombing raids. Only about a third of the merchant ships survived, and those that were left, except for some old ships of a few hundred thousand tons, had to be handed over to the Allied Powers; most of the great shipyards were dismantled and severe restrictions were imposed as to size and speed of ships that Germany was allowed to build and possess. Had it not been for the gradual lifting of these restrictions, no amount of determination and hard work could have made much difference.

By now the harbour installations have been rebuilt and extended. The merchant navy of Federal Germany with over 6 million gross tons in 1966 is not only considerably larger than before the war, but consists now of faster vessels, and the turnover of cargo handled in the German North Sea ports has surpassed the pre-war total. Recovery was most rapid in Bremen, coming more slowly in Hamburg which is particularly affected by the division of Germany and has lost about half of its pre-war hinterland.

A newcomer as a commercial port is Wilhelmshaven which was founded on virgin soil during the second half of the last century as a naval base. Since the navy was practically its only source of livelihood it was particularly hard hit after the end of the war. In the meantime, a number of industries have been attracted, though it has once again become a naval base. More important, in 1959 it had also become a major European oil port. It is linked by a main pipe-line, which reaches as far as Wesseling near Bonn, and branch lines with a number of refineries and chemical plants in the Ruhr and the northern Rhineland. Its turnover, which consists almost entirely of oil imports, was 20 million tons in 1967, making it the second largest port in Germany.

1. On the flats of the Schleswig-Holstein coast there are some tiny islands called Halligen. Life on these islets must still be very similar to what it was in the coastal zone before the dykes were built. The houses stand on man-made mounds which are just high enough to be above water level during the highest winter floods, whilst the rest of the island is covered by the waves. Because of this flooding no cultivation is possible and the land is used for grazing or hay. It seems incredible that people persist in living under such conditions, but the German farmer's attachment to the soil is so strong that he will not yield.

2. The liner *America* in berth at the Columbus quay, Bremerhaven. Situated at the mouth of the Weser, this outer port of Bremen is specially equipped to deal with passenger traffic. Note the railway terminus in the foreground and the absence of warehouses, indicating the function of this quay. Before the war Germany had large liners which several times captured the Blue Riband for the fastest crossing of the Atlantic, but she has not yet reached her former standard in this sphere. Her modern liners spend most of their time on cruises.

3. The Watten are the shallow stretches of water adjoining most of the German North Sea coast. Much of this sea was once land and it still becomes sufficiently dry at low tide to walk across to one of the islands. There, and farther out to sea, prospecting for oil is now going on and the first strike of natural gas was made in 1964.

4. A farm in eastern Friesland. Cattle are the mainstay of farming in this coastal zone. Typical also of the area is this kind of farmhouse.

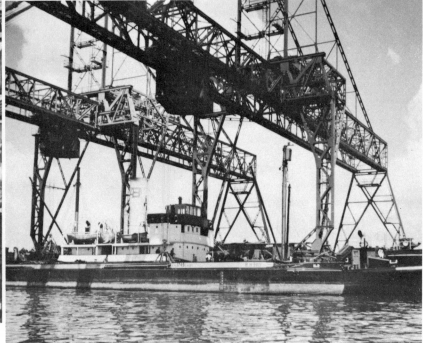

From small beginnings in an Elbe tributary, the Alster, the harbour of Hamburg has grown to its present size since about 1850. Its main advantage over British ports is the absence of closed docks, thus enabling ships to sail at any time. Although its turnover in 1968 was over 38·1 million tons of cargo, it has fallen far behind Rotterdam and Antwerp. However, Hamburg is not only a port but more than ever before a major industrial city. Not only characteristic port industries like shipbuilding, oil refining and food processing are carried on; it is also an important centre for aviation, electrical and general engineering, chemicals and printing. Shipbuilding, which has experienced a remarkable comeback since the war, is still the industry with the largest labour force; starting from scratch after 1948, ten years later Germany had overtaken Britain in tonnage launched per annum. In 1965, Germany, Britain and Sweden were nearly level with just over 1 million tons each, but far ahead was Japan which launched 5·4 million tons in the year.

Emden, with a turnover of 12·4 million tons (in 1968)—in fourth place behind Bremen—owes its rise to importance in the twentieth century to the construction of the Dortmund–Ems Canal which was opened in 1899 but is being enlarged to take the standard 1350-ton Rhine–Herne Canal barges. The original plan to turn it into the German seaport of the Rhine and Ruhr did not materialise, partly because the canal is inferior to the Rhine waterway, and partly because of a provision in the Versailles treaty and after 1945 that the other Rhine–Meuse–Scheldt ports must also be used. Nevertheless Emden's trade closely depends on the Ruhr with ore constituting over 85 per cent of its incoming cargo. Of exports, coal was its most important item (mechanical coal-loaders are shown in the picture) but this has declined. Thus the fact that it was chosen as the principal port for the export of Volkswagen cars in specially designed ships, which take 7500 cars on each voyage, was of great benefit. Since 1964 an assembly plant of the Volkswagen Works, which employs 3000 people, has broadened its formerly slender industrial base which consisted mainly of one shipyard. Another facet of its economic life is that Emden is one of the principal German home ports for herring drifters.

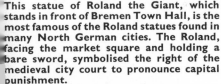

This statue of Roland the Giant, which stands in front of Bremen Town Hall, is the most famous of the Roland statues found in many North German cities. The Roland, facing the market square and holding a bare sword, symbolised the right of the medieval city court to pronounce capital punishment.

Geest and Bogs

It is the exception rather than the rule for one type of landscape to cease sharply instead of merging gradually into the next, but this is what happens in North-west Germany. The fertile *Marschen* zone ends abruptly where the land rises at the edge of the *Geest*. This term describes the entire area of the earlier moraines, as well as the sandy areas where the glacial outwash material was deposited. Once the *Marschen* people looked at the *Geest* with a certain, though scarcely justified, contempt. Although the *Geest* is not nearly so fertile, its settlement is much older and goes back some 5,000 years to the Late Stone Age; many megaliths bear witness to this early settlement.

Most of the *Geest* was then covered by mixed oak forests whose acorns provided welcome fodder for the swine of the early settlers. The settlers had other livestock also; grazing, and cutting down trees for building and firewood, thinned the forests. The better patches of soil came under the plough; and from quite early on the arable land was manured with turf which had been stripped from large areas and used as litter in the sheep-cotes. This gave the oak woods no chance to rejuvenate naturally, so that in due course vast patches became covered with heather. A special breed of sheep which could feed on heather became the agricultural mainstay until almost the entire *Geest* was a gigantic sheep-walk. Although to this day many areas of the *Geest* are called *Heide* (heath), there are only patches of heathland left now. Even on the Lüneburg Heath, the largest and best known, which a century ago was trodden by over half a million sheep, there are now only about a tenth of this number, and these are mainly kept to retain the heathland in its old state in the so-called *Heidepark*. Most of the heather has had to give way either to modern methods of farming, such as deep ploughing and the liberal application of chemical fertilisers, or to modern forestry. Today the *Geest* consists mainly of well-tended fields and meadows interspersed with large tracts of pinewoods.

It is understandable that this area did not encourage large towns; the towns that do exist are mostly on the fringes and are primarily local market centres. There are notable exceptions: Oldenburg,

Megaliths like this one—giants' "beds" or "graves" as they are called locally—were built about 5,000 years ago by the Neolithic people. The burial chamber in the foreground was originally covered by earth. They are found over the entire geest where the Quaternary glaciers had brought these large boulders from distant Scandinavia, the light soils being suitable for primitive agriculture.

Heather and juniper bushes—the latter because they are too prickly for the sheep to eat—were even as recently as fifty years ago the characteristic plants on the Lüneburg Heath. Now, as with the last flocks of sheep, they are found only in a few small areas which are purposely kept in their former state. On the whole, heather and juniper have given way to pine, rye and potato, and instead of sheep the main livestock are pigs and cattle. The traditional bee-keeping, however, is still carried on.

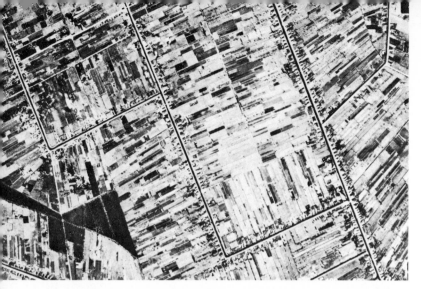

Of the many settlements in the peat bogs near the Dutch border, the town of Papenburg, shown here in a bird's-eye view, is the largest. Characteristic of these Fehnkolonien is the arrangement of the homesteads along a canal which serves for drainage and also for the transport of peat and other commodities.

Boats loaded with peat in a bog near Bremen on their way to the towns along the lower Weser where the peat is sold in the autumn. It is almost unbelievable that so close to the busy port of Bremen this scene can still be found today, exactly as it was a hundred or more years ago.

before 1918 the capital of the Grand Duchy of the same name, the centre of a region famous for its fine horses, and Lüneburg. Though not large by modern standards, the latter was of considerable importance in the fifteenth and sixteenth centuries, owing to the presence of natural springs of brine. It was also a centre of trade by virtue of its position at the head of navigation of an Elbe tributary. The brine is still turned into salt in its saltworks, but as a market it is now of local importance only. It can, however, boast many fine old buildings and tourists come to admire these witnesses of Lüneburg's former glory.

The area between the fertile *Marschen* along the coast and the equally fertile zone that fringes the Uplands in the south and the Baltic Sea in the east does not consist entirely of *Geest*: interspersed between the hills of boulder clay there are many peat bogs, large and small. The largest are found along the lower Weser and the largest of them all, the Bourtange Bog, has been for centuries the boundary which divides Germany and the Netherlands. Many bogs are also found between the lower Weser and lower Elbe. The bogs are the least tractable kind of land and they were thus the last to come under the plough. Even today there are still hundreds of square kilometres not yet cultivated. A beginning in bog reclamation was made during the twelfth century when Dutch colonists drained a stretch of the Devil's Bog near Bremen, but it was not until the eighteenth century that it started on a large scale. It was partly done by the Dutch method of first stripping the peat and then manuring and cultivating the sandy layer beneath, partly by the German way, developed later, of draining, deep ploughing and fertilising without removing the peat. In either case the landscape is characterised by a large number of canals and ditches. Even where the bog is not yet cultivated it is not without value. Peat is cut or dug for domestic fuel and for use as litter and in gardening, and until recently there was even a fairly large electric power station run on peat.

Geologically, peat is the youngest of the different types of fuel which man obtains from the earth, but because it is easily found and extracted, it was the first to be used. Even writings of classical antiquity mention that people on the North Sea coast use "mud" to feed their fires. In Germany today peat represents only a very small proportion of all the fuel providing warmth and power; the geologically older ones have come to be of great importance. Of these, mineral oil was the last to be exploited until uranium came to be used as the source of atomic energy.

Germany is not very well endowed with natural oil, but great efforts have been made, especially since 1945, to discover what oil exists. Oil production rose to nearly 8 million tons and remained at this level over the past few years, forming a declining contribution to the total amount used—80 million tons in 1967. Owing to the conditions under which oil is formed and preserved, it occurs in sedimentary basins; and over 95 per cent of the German oil comes from oilfields situated in the north-western Lowland. Two groups of oilfields are of particular importance: those on the southern fringe of the Lüneburg Heath and those near the Dutch border in the bogs west of the Ems river. The latter area, especially, used to be an economic backwater; the discovery of oil brought great benefits since it resulted in an improvement of roads and new chances of employment.

Förden and Börde

As we continue our journey into Germany away from the North Sea, we leave the *Geest* behind and come upon landscapes of different character. Eastwards, along the Kiel Canal, we reach the south-western corner of the Baltic, the region of the *Förden*, as these long and narrow inlets of the sea are called; southwards, we come to the *Börde* zone. Between the coastal stretch which is penetrated by the *Förden*, and the *Börde* zone, there are a good many differences; but there are also some similarities, of which the most important is that both regions are much more fertile than the adjoining *Geest*. In both cases this fertility is an inheritance of the last glacial period, but at this point the parallels end, since the fertility of the *Förden* zone is based on the boulder clay, whereas the *Börde* owes it to the loess. From this, further differences arise. The *Förden* zone is of pronounced relief, the steeper slopes and hill-tops are covered by beechwoods, hedgerows surround the

Glücksburg bay near Flensburg is a good example of the quiet beaches with beechwood-clad moraines in the background that are found along the Förden of Schleswig-Holstein.

The Kiel Canal at Rendsburg. This canal was built in 1887–95 and widened and deepened in 1907–14. By linking the North and Baltic Seas it not only saves much time but also makes for a safer voyage. According to the tonnage of ships passing through and the quantity of commodities on them (56 million tons in 1963), it ranks as one of the major ship canals of the world not far behind the Panama Canal where in the same year 77 million tons of goods passed through.

fields, and there are many lakes, especially in the southern part—the landscape is very varied and attractive. The *Börde* is an expanse of flat or gently sloping ground with huge fields of wheat and sugar-beet, and the skyline is broken not by trees or hedges but by the chimneys of the sugar refineries, and by large villages and towns.

In the *Förden* zone there are three major towns: Flensburg, Kiel and Lübeck. All three are or were important ports. Flensburg, a town on the Danish border, has a sizeable group of citizens of Danish mother-tongue. Of its industries rum blending and bottling holds almost a monoply in West Germany. Economically more important are its naval establishments and its market function, greatly appreciated by Danish shoppers. Kiel, now the capital of Schleswig-Holstein, is situated at the eastern entrance of the Kiel Canal and its growth was largely due to the fact that until 1945 it was the base of the German Baltic Fleet. Although Kiel suffered extensive war damage it has made a comeback. It is once more a naval base; its shipyard specialises in fishing "factory ships" and super-tankers; it has become a car ferry terminal to Scandi-

navia, a trawler port and wholesale fish market; and it too is an important shopping centre for the region and for visitors from Denmark. Lübeck, the "Queen of the Hanse", combines a well-preserved medieval appearance with modern urban vitality. Though still an important port—its turnover is the largest of any of the West German Baltic ports—industry is nowadays its main economic prop. It can even boast some of the few blast-furnaces in West Germany situated away from both coalfields and local iron ore, though others were recently built at Bremen.

The *Börde* is not only a very fertile region; it also possesses important raw materials: rock salt, potash salt, iron ore, brown coal and even a little coal. These resources, together with the requirements of agriculture and its location on both main railway lines and the Mittelland Canal, have made it an important industrial region. Hanover, the capital of Lower Saxony, is the largest of the towns. It originated as a bridge town at the head of navigation on a Weser tributary and, being at the junction of many routes, it became the largest industrial centre—the West German Industrial

Wiped out by air raids, the centre of Kiel has risen again. The Howaldt-Deutsche Werft shipyard which is an important part of its economic life can be seen on the distant bank of the Förde, but only one building of medieval origin remains, the "Nikolai" church (on the right of the picture). As a port with a turnover of about 1 million tons (mostly imports) Kiel ranks well after Lübeck.

Lübeck is a city with a great past. Founded in the twelfth century it became the centre of the German Baltic trade and the "Queen of the Hanse". The might and wealth it once possessed are still clearly visible everywhere on a walk through the old town on its island site. Even from the air one can see the large churches, the old merchant houses and warehouses along the river bank, and the famous Holsten Gate (in the left foreground). The turnover of the port in 1967 was 4½ million tons.

The old market square in Brunswick. Although it is now a modern industrial city, Brunswick has preserved many features of the period when it was the residence of the Dukes of Lower Saxony.

Fair is held here. Hanover has very varied industries: food processing, engineering, the chemical (fertilisers), vehicle and rubber industries (it has the largest tyre plant on the Continent). Nevertheless, thanks to imaginative rebuilding after much war damage, it has remained very attractive. Brunswick, at one time a ducal residence, has preserved many medieval features, despite much war damage, and it is a centre of the canning and sugar industries, while vehicle building, engineering, the optical industry and publishing are other important facets of its economic life.

In great contrast to these old centres of trade and manufacture are two new towns which have developed on virgin soil since 1938. One is Salzgitter, the home of the iron and steel combine of that name; the other is Wolfsburg, the home of the Volkswagen plant. Both these towns are still in the making. The former, after a growth period, is in a state of crisis resulting from difficulties in the steel industry which made use of the local low grade ore uneconomic. The latter is still growing vigorously on the strength of the motor industry boom.

The Salzgitter iron and steel combine, although one of the largest German works of its kind, is nevertheless one of their more recent. There are two earlier ironworks near by—at Peine and Ilsede—but the large-scale utilisation of these most extensive German iron ore deposits with reserves of 2,000 million tons began as late as 1937. Almost annihilated by the post-war dismantling programme which left the works with only three out of its former twelve blast-furnaces and deprived it of its entire steel-making and further processing potential, they began to expand again in 1950. Now the combine has seven blast-furnaces, two steel plants with a potential of $1\frac{1}{2}$ million tons, two rolling mills, a foundry, a nitrogen plant, power station and several engineering works. The Salzgitter concern comprises in addition to its own sources of iron ore, mines in South Germany (Amberg), coal-mines in the Ruhr, oil-wells, a major shipyard (Howaldtwerke, Kiel), engineering works in Berlin and factories producing rolling-stock and heavy lorries—a classic example of vertical integration. The total labour force of the concern is nearly 80,000 with over 12,000 of these in Salzgitter itself. The plant at Salzgitter is served by a branch of the Mittelland Canal, completed in 1938, which has the capacity to take 1000-ton barges and links the waterways of the Rhine and Elbe systems. The works obtain their coal by canal from the Ruhr. This accounts for the large turnover of its harbour, which with over 2 million tons in 1967 was the largest of any on this canal.

Salzgitter itself, which became a municipality in 1942, is a strange and unique town. Well over half of its area consists of agricultural land, and the twenty-nine component settlements, most of them former villages, are widely separated from each other.

Bird's-eye view of the Volkswagen car plant and part of the town of Wolfsburg. Both were founded on virgin soil in 1938, the town taking its name from the country house just visible in the clump of trees at the centre right of the picture. The main reasons for the choice of site were the almost central location within the German Reich, and proximity to major communication lines and the Salzgitter steelworks. Coal for the power station which supplies the works and the town (located on the right-hand side of the factory front at least 1 km long) is brought by barge on the Mittelland Canal. (It runs from left to right in the picture between the works area and the town centre.) After considerable war damage the works had to start practically from scratch in 1948—much help was given by the British occupation authorities but as a consequence of the division of Germany, the original locational advantages no longer apply. It has had to obtain its sheet steel from farther afield as Salzgitter steel was found to be not quite suitable, and although the car manufacturers of the Western Allies who could have obtained the patents thought the unconventional design of "the beetle" had no future, the Volkswagen concern has become the largest car manufacturers outside the United States and in value of turnover, the leading German firm. By 1965 it had produced more than 10 million vehicles.

About half of the total labour force of over 100,000 is employed in the principal plant at Wolfsburg, the other 50,000 in branch factories at Brunswick, Emden, Hanover, Kassel and Ingolstadt where Volkswagen acquired control of the Auto-Union motor works. An additional 18,600 work in factories and assembly plants abroad in Australia, Brazil, Mexico and South Africa.

In 1965 the West German motor industry produced nearly 3 million cars—taking second place after the U.S.A.—and over 50 per cent of these were made by the Volkswagen concern. Perhaps more important still is that nearly 60 per cent of their total production was exported.

Backed by the success of Volkswagen it is not surprising that the town of Wolfsburg grew very rapidly. The picture can only give an inadequate impression of the town planning. A town centre with excellent progressive shopping facilities and ample parking space, architecturally distinguished town hall, civic centre and theatre, is surrounded by neighbourhood units which are separated from each other by stretches of woodland and occasionally artificial lakes. (See centre right of the picture.) A distinctive difference from the new towns in Britain is the emphasis of living in blocks of flats (heated by district heating). A feature peculiar to Wolfsburg is the virtual absence of garages despite an extremely high degree of motorisation. This is not a planning mistake but done on purpose as the air-cooled Volkswagen can "live out" happily in parking bays.

6. The Northern Rhineland and Westphalia

Politically this region is almost coincident with the **Land North Rhine-Westphalia**.

Major cities (in thousands) arranged according to number of inhabitants in 1939:

	1939	1968
Cologne (*Köln*)	772·2	853·9
Essen	666·7	702·3
Dortmund	542·3	646·4
Düsseldorf	541·4	686·1
Duisburg	434·6	465·1
Wuppertal	401·7	412·2
Gelsenkirchen	317·6	354·8
Bochum	305·5	346·8
Oberhausen	191·8	251·0
Krefeld	171·0	224·8
Aachen	162·2	176·2
Hagen	151·8	199·7
Münster	141·1	202·8
Solingen	140·5	173·9
Mülheim	137·5	189·5
Bielefeld	129·5	168·9
Mönchengladbach	128·5	151·8
Bonn*	108·8	138·1
Osnabrück	107·1	140·0
Remscheid	103·9	133·7
Herne	94·7	102·5
Wanne-Eickel	86·6	101·0
Recklinghausen	86·3	126·1
Bottrop	83·4	109·5
Rheydt	77·3	99·9
Witten	73·6	97·2
Wattenscheid	61·5	80·4
Neuss	59·7	114·3
Gladbeck	58·7	82·3
Castrop-Rauxel	56·6	84·4
Leverkusen	50·1	107·1

*In 1969 Bad Godesberg was incorporated into Bonn, increasing the number of its inhabitants by over 70,000.

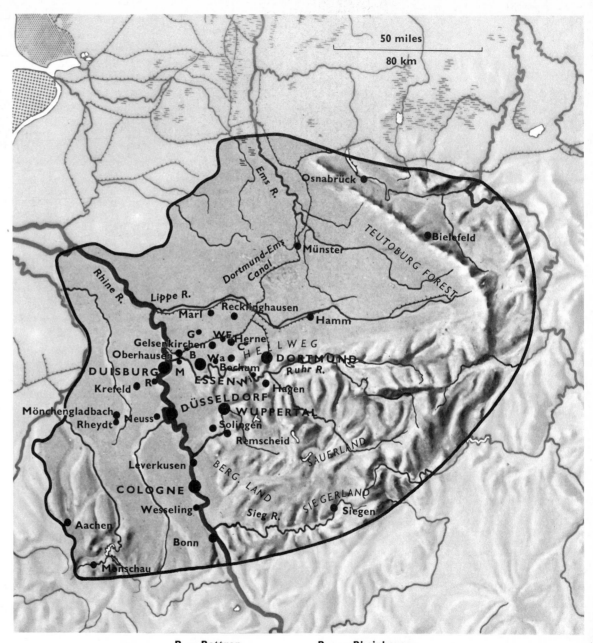

B = Bottrop	**R** = Rheinhausen
C = Castrop-Rauxel	**WE** = Wanne-Eickel
G = Gladbeck	**Wa** = Wattenscheid
M = Mülheim	**Wi** = Witten

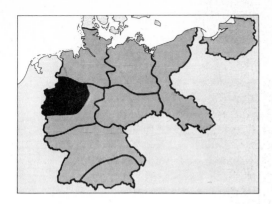

Important though industry is in most parts of Germany, there can be no doubt that in this region lies Germany's industrial heart and that the gigantic Ruhr coalfield has been the most significant single factor in its industrial development.

Coal and Iron—the Ruhr Region Proper

On the northern flank of the Middle Rhine Highlands, there lie coal-bearing beds of great thickness, which dip away from the Uplands, to disappear beneath the later deposits of the North German Lowland. Only on the southern fringe do the coal seams of the Ruhr coalfield reach the surface and it was here, where they are further laid bare by the Ruhr river, that coal-mining began in the Middle Ages. The amount of coal mined, however, remained extremely small and, although around the middle of the last century the seeds which led to its future greatness had begun to germinate, the countryside was still essentially a rural one. The

growth started in earnest in the 1870s, following the foundation of the German Empire, and was based not on the exposed coal measures but on that part of the coalfield to the north of the Ruhr river where the coal was "concealed" by later deposits. Although this made mining more costly it was amply repaid since the most valuable coal occurs here, coal best suited to coking and thus for use in the blast-furnaces. In the northernmost part of the coalfield there is another type of coal which it was worth while mining from a depth exceeding 1,000 metres; this is the so-called "gas coal" which, because of its high gas-content, was used as a raw material in the chemical industry.

The reason why different types of coal are mined at different parts of the coalfield is that the coal seams not only dip northwards but at the same time also increase in thickness. In the southern part of the coalfield the upper layers, which contain gas coal and coking coal, were eroded away during earlier geological periods and only the less valuable anthracitic coal, suitable merely for fuel, remained. This richness in the most valuable types of coal, and the great diversity of types of coal found in one single field, were advantages enjoyed by the Ruhr coalfield; difficulties and thus high costs of mining have, however, largely wiped these out.

Another characteristic of the Ruhr coalfield is the absence of the extensive areas of derelict land which are so frequently associated with coal-mining. The chief reasons are the late starting date of large-scale mining and the great resources

contained in the coalfield—64 thousand million tons—which will allow mining to continue for as long as coal is likely to be needed. Neither are there any derelict canals. The canals of the Ruhr region date from the turn of the century and later; they were built of sufficient size to compete with the railways and are amongst the busiest inland waterways of Germany. Slag-heaps, too, are almost absent since the waste is usually filled back into the worked-out sections of the mines; those that do exist, and the abandoned part of the coalfield, have been reafforested.

One unique feature is the close juxtaposition of industry and farming. Especially where coal-mining has invaded the fertile *Hellweg*, a part of the *Börde* zone, intensive agriculture continues between the pits and the built-up areas. Even the towns are not wholly unattractive, as is usual in industrial regions. Some Ruhr towns can look back to a long history before industrialisation began and have carefully preserved their most valuable features. Because industrial development was comparatively late, even at the outset housing was of a better quality than in the coalfields affected by the early stages of the Industrial Revolution; provision was made for parks and open spaces and the miners and other workers were housed in pleasantly laid out estates.

Although the earliest ironworks used charcoal, coking coal became the basis on which the gigantic iron and steel industry of the Ruhr could develop. At first local ores like bog ore and the carboniferous blackband ore were used, but these soon became exhausted. Ores were then brought in from farther afield: the Siegerland and the Lahn-Dill mines to the south, the Lorraine and Luxembourg iron-ore fields, from Spain and especially Sweden, and even from overseas, North Africa and Labrador. Much of this ore was, and still is, brought to the ironworks by barges, and there was also a considerable coal export —although this has declined during the post-war period.

Nowhere else in Germany are there so many large cities (altogether about thirty) in such close proximity. Industrial cities though they all are now, they differ greatly in origin. Some have medieval roots and have even preserved their core of medieval buildings, like Recklinghausen, the northernmost to be overwhelmed by industry. Others, like Herne, have nothing but the name in common with the village or hamlet from which they started, and others still, like Oberhausen, grew up around a railway station where not even a hamlet of that name had existed previously. Common to all is the

tremendous pace of their growth and two of them, Dortmund, famous not only for its iron and steel industry but also for its beer, and Essen, the "metropolis of the Ruhr", have populations of more than half a million. Duisburg is the western cornerstone of the great Ruhr conurbation. Situated where the River Ruhr and— what is more significant today—the Rhine–Herne Canal join the Rhine, it has grown into the greatest inland port of Europe, and by being closest to the source of ore into Germany's leading town for iron and copper smelting and steel-making. The Thyssen combine is here, the biggest steel company of Europe by far.

The growth of Essen is closely linked with the industrial fortunes of the Krupp family. At the time when the first Krupp workshop, an iron foundry, was established in 1811, Essen had about 8,000 inhabitants. By 1939 its population had grown to over 600,000 and of these about 270,000 were directly dependent on the Krupp concern, being either employees or members of their families.

The harbour of Duisburg–Ruhrort is so large that only a small section can be shown here. (Its turnover in 1968 was 39·4 million tons.) A remarkable undertaking in progress is mining beneath the harbour to produce subsidence and lower the basins by about 2 metres to the level of the Rhine, which has deepened its bed by that amount since about 1900.

The old Ruhr towns have treasured their medieval buildings like this ancient church in the heart of Essen.

Though Krupp was the best-known firm of the Ruhr there were several similar ones, the tendency being towards integration into extremely large enterprises. After the war an attempt was made by the Allied Powers to split these up but they have formed again.

Nevertheless, much has changed and is changing. An important chemical industry, originally based on coke-oven by-products, had grown up in some of the old-established industrial towns like Gelsenkirchen. Later, coal itself was used as raw material and shortly before the Second World War one of the first German new towns, Marl, was founded in connection with the establishment of a large chemical plant. The main products of the chemical industry were originally dyes, but during the later 1930s synthetic petrol and lubricants as well as buna—synthetic rubber—became most important. After 1945 synthetic fibres and plastics had become important new products. The hydrogenation plants became refineries, and the other chemical plants used oil as their raw material basis, as this was much more economic than coal.

The large-scale change-over to the use of oil as fuel has further reduced the demand for coal and has brought about a difficult situation. Even the increase in iron and steel production has not helped very much. Modern metallurgical methods have drastically reduced the fuel requirement of the industry. Only one use of coal has been increasing—its transformation into electric current in giant power stations. Production of electric current, which in the area of the present Federal Republic had amounted to 37,000 million kilowatt hours in 1938, had in 1967 reached 184,680 million kilowatt hours. However future expansion will be largely on the basis of nuclear energy rather than coal. Still, this use, together with the demand for metallurgical coke, does provide a sound basis for coal-mining, but as it is a limited one the closure of mines with a total annual capacity of almost 50 million tons could not be avoided. (The total West German production of coal declined from a peak of 152 million tons in 1956 to 112 million tons in 1967.) Those Ruhr towns, amongst them Bottrop, to whom mining was virtually the only economic prop, are going through a particularly difficult period, but nearly all towns are affected to some extent and are trying to attract new industries. Most successful so far has been undoubtedly Bochum which persuaded the Opel Motor Co. (a subsidiary of General Motors) to establish two branch factories giving work to more than 12,000 people. Other developments at Bochum are the establishment of an "out-of-town shopping centre" on the American pattern, and a large new university. Another university has been founded at Dortmund.

As long ago as 1927 all the cities and districts of the Ruhr joined together to a single planning region, and the planning authorities are doing their utmost to make the region attractive to people and new industries, for instance by the designation of "green belts" between the individual conurbations and by improving the road network. The Ruhr region is far from worn out and has many advantages for the establishment of new industries. It will certainly weather the storm, but it will no longer be the region with an economic life dominated by the products for which it became famous, coal and steel, but an industrial region of infinite complexity ready to face the challenge of the twenty-first century.

The Ruhr coalfield extends to the left bank of the Rhine where at Rheinhausen it supplies coal to one of the most modern German steel plants; this too is part of the Krupp "empire". Having risen from the ruins like a phoenix to the biggest German private firm with a labour force of over 100,000, Krupp with his many coal-mines was hit particularly hard by the coal crisis and the economic recession of 1966–7. The State had to come to the rescue and the firm was turned into a limited company.

No other region of Germany can boast so many reservoirs as the Bergische Land and Sauerland, east of Cologne. Even so the industrial and domestic demand for water is constantly increasing and additional reservoirs are still being constructed.

The Upland Fringe

Of the numerous problems posed by such a tremendous concentration of heavy industries and people one of the most important is that of the water-supply. In this the Ruhr region is particularly fortunate since the hills of the German Uplands rise immediately to the south and east of it and, being the first heights in the way of the rain-bearing westerlies, they receive a particularly high rainfall. Although industry has now deserted the Ruhr Valley and shifted northwards, the name "Ruhr region" is not only justified on historical grounds but also because this district could never have reached its present importance without the water of the Ruhr river, which rises in the hills of the Sauerland (a corrupted form of sou'(th) land). Even so, the natural flow of the river, varying as it does throughout the year, would be quite insufficient to satisfy the demand for water; the surplus water from periods of high rainfall must be saved and this is done by a great number of barrages on the Ruhr itself and on its headwaters. Amongst these is the famous Möhne Dam.

In its landscape the thinly settled higher parts of the Sauerland, with its extensive forests, are a far cry from the teeming Ruhr region, and yet functionally they are a part of it. Not only do they supply the "life-blood" of the industry; they are also the source of a large proportion of pit props and a recreation ground for the workers and town-dwellers of the Ruhr.

The hill country to the west of the high Sauerland is an industrial region in its own right and of much longer standing than the Ruhr; but not being located on a coalfield it has not developed into a great industrial conurbation, and attractive woods, fields and meadows still separate the various industrial centres from one another. Despite its age it has been overshadowed by the Ruhr and is now greatly dependent upon it in many respects. The iron industry of the Siegerland, based on local iron ore and going back to early historic times, is still of some importance though it has passed its heyday. The demand for charcoal gave rise to a very strange type of agriculture, a regular rotation between arable cultivation and oak coppice, but this is now a thing of the past and the iron industry relies for its blast-furnaces on Ruhr coal which it obtains as return freight for artificially enriched iron ore. Manufacturing is highly specialised and concentrates on the production of tinplate, but there are also foundries and engineering plants.

The economy of the Bergische Land, situated between the Siegerland and the Ruhr, is even more dependent on the Ruhr region. Two types of industry—cutlery, tools and hardware on the one hand and textiles on the other—are of long standing, whereas the chemical and pharmaceutical industry is a relative newcomer.

The local iron industry dates back to the Middle Ages, relying as it did on local ore and the swift streams which were harnessed for hammering and grinding. Today it depends on iron, steel and coal from the Ruhr, and the water power is no longer used directly but in the form of electricity. It has, however, largely preserved one characteristic feature: cottage-type industry still prevails and large factories are the exception. Its world-famous centres are the two cities of Solingen and Remscheid, situated on the plateau tops at opposite sides of the deep Wupper valley. Solingen specialises in cutlery and Remscheid in all kinds of tools and also skates.

Larger than both these cities together is Wuppertal, a town situated farther upstream in the valley of the Wupper. This city was once two towns and has existed under its present name only since 1930. It is, and has been since the sixteenth century, chiefly concerned with textiles, but while its chief activity was then linen spinning and weaving, it is now synthetic fibre manufacture, as well as the weaving of carpets and furnishing fabrics. Of more recent date are its chemical and engineering industries, the latter specialising in textile machines.

In its layout Wuppertal is much influenced by its site at the bottom of the V-shaped valley. The expansion of the two towns from which the present city originated resulted in a "ribbon town" of little width but of a length of about 16 kilometres. A town of such a shape poses serious traffic problems, but for public transport these were solved by the construction of an overhead railway hanging above the river.

The industrial region of the hill country on the right bank of the Rhine finds a parallel in the foothills of the Eifel between the Rhine and the Belgian frontier. Industry is again concerned largely with

The most widely known feature of the city of Wuppertal is its overhead railway—an engineer's space-saving solution. Its synthetic fibre plant with a labour force of nearly 30,000 is the earliest established and largest in the world.

Aachen's jewel is its cathedral, the octagonal centre part of which dates from the time of Charles the Great and contains the tomb of this famous ruler.

iron, steel and textiles, but the area differs in one important respect from the regions south of the Ruhr. While the ores which originally supported the iron industry have become exhausted, there is a local supply of coal in the Aachen coalfield.

The textile industry has long specialised in woollen cloth and finds its greatest concentration in Aachen, the leading "woollen town" of Germany. Aachen was earlier famed for its hot springs—its name means "at the waters"—already known to the Romans who founded the forerunner of the present city. Its major claim to historical fame is that Charles the Great made it his favourite residence.

The Lowland Bays

Between the western and eastern foothills of the Middle Rhine Highlands, the Northern Lowland stretches in a "bay" along the Rhine as far as Bonn. This is a favoured piece of country endowed with many treasures. Its earlier history was greatly influenced by its sheltered position and its fertile soils: loess in the higher southern part, and loam covering the gravel terraces of the north. These advantages gave rise to and still support intensive agriculture: wheat and sugar-beet and also market-gardening in the southern part and cattle north of the Ruhr mouth. From about this point the Rhine is confined in its flood plain by dykes and the landscape, with its many canals, closely resembles a polder region.

Agricultural land covers most of the area. In the south rural settlement is concentrated in villages, in the north isolated farmsteads prevail; but nature has endowed this region with some mineral resources also: potash and common salt, and, most important, brown coal, which occurs in the southern bay west of Cologne. Only the easternmost part of this vast field is being exploited so far, that part where in the Ville ridge the brown coal occurs close enough to the surface to be mined by the open-pit process. (This differs from open-cast in that huge pits are excavated and then reclaimed after the coal has been extracted.) These fields contribute by far the greatest part of the 100 million tons or so of brown coal mined in West Germany. Brown coal-mining has been highly mechanised for a long time, but the development after 1945 has seen a change from the traditional use

Düsseldorf, the capital of North Rhine-Westphalia, is an attractive modern city with many open spaces. Its shops in the Königsallee are famous all over Germany.

The birthplace of Bonn's most famous son: Ludwig van Beethoven.

Although Bonn has become the capital of the Federal Republic of Germany, the vegetable market is still held in front of the town hall. Nevertheless, its life is not quite so provincial as its nickname "Federal Capital Village" implies.

situated some distance from the Rhine it had its boundaries adjusted and thus became a Rhine town with its own harbour. Its economy has kept pace with its territorial expansion and now embraces other types of textile manufacturing, engineering, chemical and food industries.

Mönchengladbach is an old city, owing its present size to its central position in the cotton industry of the lower Rhine. It too has diversified its interests and now specialises in textile machinery, among other engineering products.

The Northern Lowland not only extends along the Rhine to the south. East of the lower Rhine there is another such extension of the Lowland, the Münster Bay. Apart from its south-western section which has been absorbed into the Ruhr region, the Münster Bay is still agricultural, with isolated farms and hamlets in the northern part, larger villages in the south, and every now and then a country town serving as a market centre. The best soils occur in the south, the loess zone of the Westphalian *Börde*; there agriculture is at its most intensive. One crop of particular importance is barley, greatly in demand with the large breweries of Dortmund. The heart of the region, the Münsterland to the north of the *Börde*, is not quite as fertile; a typical landscape contains meadows, pastures and fields, and impressive groups of trees. Occasionally on sandy stretches we find patches of pine forests or even heath interspersed with the farmland. This is a landscape which hardly changed for some hundreds of years. Not that farming is backward here, but it is farming which is proud of its tradition, "peasant" farming in the best sense, efficient, and far more a way of life than merely an occupation.

An ancient farm in Westphalia. Often standing on its own and surrounded by a ditch, a Westphalian farmhouse makes us realise that it is not only an Englishman to whom "his home is his castle".

The high street of Münster, flattened in an air raid, has been rebuilt. As in many other towns which suffered a similar fate, an attempt was made to re-create much of the old atmosphere without actually copying what had been lost.

Less fertile than the south and the centre of the Münster Bay are its western and eastern sections. In the west, which adjoins the Netherlands, there is much sand and marshland. The proximity of Holland is responsible for the characteristic industries of the border towns—processing of cotton and tobacco—which are an extension of the Dutch ones and there is much daily commuting across the border.

The city of Münster lies in the centre of the Bay and serves as its regional focus. Founded at the time of Charles the Great as a bishop's see, it still fulfils this function; for the Münsterland was until 1802 a prince-bishopric, and like the Rhineland (in contrast to the rest of North Germany) it remained Roman Catholic during the Reformation. Since the late eighteenth century it has also been a university city. Its main function today is to be the chief grain, timber and cattle market of the Bay, a position for which the closeness of the Dortmund–Ems Canal particularly fits it. Its small- and medium-scale industries are varied, since their purpose is largely to serve the region by processing agricultural products and providing various types of machinery.

Also part of Westphalia is the Teutoburg Forest and its northern foreland. This northernmost outpost of the German Uplands, rising as it does from the low-lying Münster Bay to about 300 metres, gives a more wall-like impression than its actual height would suggest. Despite its name it is not a continuous stretch of forest; the oak, beech and fir woods are confined to the ridges while the valleys in between have been cleared for agriculture. The Teutoburg Forest was never a great obstacle to communication since it is transected by through-valleys. At the northern approaches to these "gates" a number of cities developed, the most important of them being Bielefeld, a busy industrial town, centre of the West German linen industry, and Osnabrück, an important traffic junction, which has numerous industries. To these, local supplies of iron ore and a small coalfield were a stimulus to industrial development.

A scene in the Teutoburg Forest, known to every schoolchild in Germany as the place where the Roman legions were decisively defeated by an alliance of Teutonic tribes in A.D. 9. There is a huge monument to their leader, Armenius, on the distant hill to the right of the picture.

7. The Middle Rhine Highlands and the Hesse and Weser Hills

Politically this region consists of the northern parts of the Länder Rhineland-Palatinate and Hesse.

Major cities (in thousands) arranged according to number of inhabitants in 1939:

	1939	1968
Kassel	216·1	212·5
Koblenz	91·1	105·4
Trier	88·1	104·7
Göttingen	51·2	112·6
Giessen	46·6	73·5

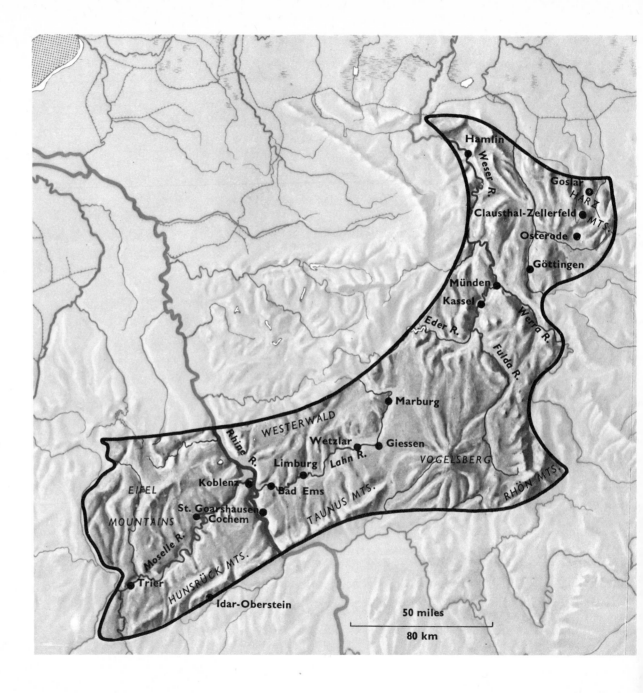

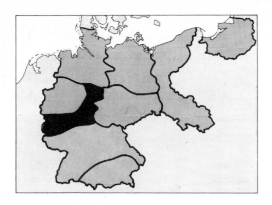

Few people, whatever their personal preferences, would dare to grade Germany's landscapes. Yet all would surely agree in rating this region very highly. Here, man and nature have achieved a rare harmony, a union whose mellow perfection is emphasised by contrast—sheltered valleys vie with exposed, windswept heights, their leached and meagre soils so different from the fertile vales.

The Middle Rhine Highlands

The Rhine and its tributaries, the Moselle and Lahn, divide the Middle Rhine Highlands, geologically a single mountain group, into its geographical units: Hunsrück and Taunus in the south, Eifel and Westerwald in the north. It is only from the valleys, especially the Rhine–Main plain into which the Taunus drops steeply, that the Middle Rhine Highlands look like "mountains". On the top they usually give the impression of being an undulating high plateau only occasionally dominated by tall outcrops of quartzite or volcanic rocks whose hardness resists denudation. In the Eifel there are also about fifty volcanic cones consisting of slag; these have survived because of the short time (in geological terms) that has elapsed since their formation during the later part of the Ice Age. Even more recent, dating from the early post-glacial period, are the *Maare* of the Eifel, the round lakes which now fill the craters of gas explosions. Vestiges of former volcanic activity are the many hot and other mineral springs which have given rise to countless spas, large and small. No other region of Germany can boast so many names containing the word "*Bad*" (spa).

The volcanic features are also of economic importance. Not only do they enhance the scenery and attract many visitors to, for example, the Siebengebirge (the Seven Mountains), south-east of Bonn, but the basalt of which they are made is a most valuable stone. It is widely quarried for paving stones and for use as a road metal, and is unequalled for millstones and as a facing material for sea dykes. (The most important sea dykes of the Netherlands use Rhenish basalt for this purpose.) Volcanic ash, which was thickly deposited in the Rhine basin north of Koblenz, is also quarried. On it is based the manufacture of a light yet strong building stone which has been much used in the post-war building boom in West Germany.

There are other valuable resources in the ground, particularly in the Westerwald. Although not very extensive they are important because they provide an income to supplement the farming which is carried out under generally adverse conditions. Brown coal deposits, preserved under sheet lava, have here to be reached by deep mining; there is also some iron ore which gave rise to a small iron industry, and excellent clay deposits east of Koblenz have long been used in making pottery. The working of semi-precious stones in Idar–Oberstein in the Hunsrück stemmed from the local raw material, agate, but now relies on imports from India and Brazil and also on synthetic stones, which are at least in part manufactured locally.

The greatest wealth of this region and the most beautiful scenery are, however, found in its valleys.

The Rhine Valley itself offers countless beautiful views. For over a thousand years the slopes have been painstakingly terraced to make the famous vineyards which are only now and then interrupted by rock precipices, crowned by medieval castles, or by woods in parts where there is too much shade. Many small towns owe their existence to the wine trade. Often on Roman sites and still full of medieval buildings, they line the valley of the Rhine on either bank, attracting great numbers of tourists, who come to sample the local produce and to join in the gay wine harvest festivals in the autumn.

A pleasant pastime is to watch the many ships which ply up or down stream, but for their navigators this is the most treacherous part of the Rhine and in one section it is even necessary to take on a pilot. Many people even outside Germany know the song of the beautiful Lorelei who made the skipper forget to steer his boat so that it was wrecked—a cruel reminder of the frequent shipwrecks which occurred before a proper navigation channel was blasted in 1834.

The only big town on the middle Rhine is Koblenz, situated at the confluence of the Rhine and the Moselle. Almost opposite, on the right bank, the Rhine is joined by the River Lahn and this gives Koblenz the advantage of being at a river "cross-roads". Here you will find the only bridges across the Rhine in the stretch from Mainz to Bonn, and the main function of Koblenz is to serve as the regional administrative, shopping and business centre. Close by there is the building material industry using volcanic ash mentioned in chapter 3; there is also a small iron industry.

The valley of the Moselle (another name of Latin origin—*Mosella*, the little Mosa, i.e. Meuse) is the longest of the tributary valleys of the Rhine and is in many respects similar to it. Here, too, the slopes are covered by vineyards and there are many ancient towns and villages. The oldest of these is Trier, situated at the point where the Moselle enters Germany. It is not only a former Roman town but was before that the capital of a Celto-Teuton tribe after whom the Romans named it *Colonia Treverorum*. The most important of all Roman towns on German soil, it was even the imperial summer residence between A.D. 285 and 400. Impressive buildings remain, the largest extant north of the Alps, the Porta Nigra (the north gate of the Roman town wall), the Basilica and the ruins of the imperial baths and the amphitheatre. Trier has the distinction of being one of the earliest German ecclesiastical centres, and many buildings, like the Elector's Palace, date from the period when the archbishop was also territorial ruler.

The volcanic cones in the south-eastern Eifel Mountains, of which some are shown here in this scene not far from Koblenz, were formed when Palaeolithic man had already come to these regions. These volcanic slag heaps rising above the plateau are also distinguished from the surrounding agricultural land by their cover of woods or scrub.

A peasant's cottage in the Eifel, a reminder of the difficult physical conditions and the custom of divided inheritance which reduced the size of holdings to below family subsistence level and were responsible for the Eifel becoming one of the depressed areas of Germany, with much seasonal and also permanent emigration. Various government measures such as reallocation of land and reafforestation, as well as tourism, have helped to combat much of the former poverty.

Of the many spas owing their existence to various mineral springs, Bad Ems on the Lahn is probably the most famous, being among the best known in Europe. The mineral waters of a number of these places are bottled and can be bought almost anywhere in West Germany. Moreover, Bad Ems has even gained a place in the political history of Europe for the fateful "Ems telegram" of 13 July 1870 which precipitated the Franco-Prussian War. The contents of the telegram, in which the King of Prussia informed Bismarck of the proceedings of a meeting with the French Ambassador, was released to the Press by Bismarck in a judiciously altered statement, and its publication so incensed France that she decided to declare war on Prussia—as Bismarck had calculated and hoped.

In the Rhine Gorge there is little space left for the road and the double-track railway which follow each bank of the river. The Rhine Valley has been an important trade route since the Middle Ages and this, and the demands of the wine trade, gave rise to many small towns, like St. Goarshausen (on the right bank—i.e. the eastern bank), using the little space as best they could. Note also the contrast in land use between the valley sides and the Taunus high plateau, and also between the north and south facing slope of the tributary valley, illustrating the importance of aspect for viticulture.

Harvest in the Taunus. Rising abruptly from the deeply incised valleys large parts of the high plateau are used for agriculture whereas the valley slopes and the summit hills, which consist of harder rocks like quartzite, are covered by woodlands. Although this was originally an area of broad-leaf forest and beech woods still predominate, conifers have gained in importance since about 1800.

No city north of the Alps can show its link with Roman times by such impressive remains as Trier. What other modern high street is dominated by a Roman gate? The *porta nigra* (in the centre of the picture) was the largest of all the gateways in the Roman Empire.

From the planting of the vine in the spring to the moment when we can raise the fragrant drink in a toast, much water flows down the Rhine and much hard labour and skill is expended. After planting it takes three years for a young plant to produce its first grapes and in the meantime the vines have to be pruned, trained, sprayed and manured. Because the quality of the wine depends on the weather, each year's financial gain is subject to more variation than in any other branch of agriculture. The stones on the ground in the picture store the heat and keep the soil warm overnight.

As a line of communication, however, the Moselle Valley is quite unlike that of the Rhine. The river winds so much that its course from Trier to Koblenz is twice as long as a straight line between these towns. The main road and railway therefore follow the valley only in its lowest section. In order to reduce transport costs of Ruhr coal to the Lorraine blast-furnaces, France had for a long time urged its canalisation. In 1956 the government of the Federal Republic of Germany agreed and construction was completed as soon as 1964. To what extent the existence of this modern waterway will change the economic geography of the Moselle Valley itself is as yet difficult to gauge. The barrages with their locks and hydroelectric power stations have certainly taken away some of its romantic atmosphere.

The Lahn Valley differs from both of the others. Only in its lowest part is it gorge-like and meandering. Vineyards no longer predominate; their place is taken by woods. Settlement is more intermittent and is concentrated in the wider valley sections such as the basin of Limburg. Farther upstream is Wetzlar, with an iron and steel industry based on the local ore, but known the world over for its optical industry (Leitz plant). As far as Wetzlar the Lahn has been made navigable for 180-ton barges, the main freight being limestone quarried west of Limburg which is shipped to the Ruhr for use in the blast-furnaces.

East of Wetzlar we leave the Middle Rhine Highlands and its valleys and come to an area different in appearance and character.

As in the Rhine Gorge the steep valley sides of the Moselle have been extensively terraced for centuries in this cradle of Germany's viticulture. Moselle wine is generally lighter than Rhine wine, though in no way inferior. Hock, the English generic term for Rhine wine, is actually a misnomer, as it is derived from Hochheim a place on the lower Main river.

Eltz Castle, situated on a narrow rock ledge in a tributary valley of the lower Moselle, is not only the most beautifully sited of the many local castles but one of the best preserved medieval castles of Germany as a whole.

The "Deutsches Eck" (German corner) at the confluence of the Moselle and the Rhine at Koblenz. Like so many of the Rhenish towns Koblenz is built on the site of a Roman settlement and its name is derived from the Latin _Confluentes_ (river junctions).

A view of the lower Lahn Valley above Bad Ems. In this part of the valley there are some vineyards, but in contrast to the Moselle Valley they are confined to the most favourable sites and viticulture plays only a subordinate role in the economy.

The Vale and Hills of Hesse and the Weser Hills

In its structure, this region is the northward continuation of the line of the Rhine Rift Valley, and routeways to the north take advantage of the gap it makes through the Uplands. It is, however, an area of great geological diversity, and the variety of rocks gives rise to rapid changes of scenery. Most of the region is underlain by sandstones and limestones of Triassic age, but there are also areas of much younger rocks; outcrops of basalt occur everywhere except in the very north and further help to diversify the landscape. The main contrast is that between the wooded heights and the fertile loess-covered vales with their ancient settlements, characteristic of which are the large nucleated villages. Favoured by soil and climate, agriculture is very intensive, a fact clearly indicated by the cultivation of wheat and sugar-beet.

Where settlement advanced to the hills during the great medieval clearing period, agriculture is of a different kind. The greater amount of rainfall which the Vogelsberg (the largest continuous area of basalt in Europe) receives because of its height, is emphasised by the impermeability of the rock; arable farming gives way to animal husbandry. But even this barely affords sufficient livelihood and many farmers have to augment their income by other work, as for instance, in the numerous quarries. In the Rhön Mountains, too, the agricultural economy is dominated by the volcanic heights, although their base is formed of Triassic rocks. This situation was aggravated by a fragmentation of holdings, and the Rhön Mountains were until recently a land of the poor, with people turning for employment to the quarries, or to cottage industries, such as wood-carving, basket and straw-hat making, and knitting. Some people find work as far away as the Ruhr and there is a good deal of seasonal emigration. The tourist trade (in summer the Rhön is a centre of glider flying and in winter there is ski-ing) has, however, helped to improve the local economy.

The region is not well endowed with mineral resources. There are the sandstone and basalt quarries, and some brown coal deposits worked partly by open pit, partly by deep mining. In the northern part there are also some salt- and potash-mines, but the small coal-mines near Hamlin have closed down.

Of the many old towns rich in medieval buildings, only one, Kassel, has developed into a major industrial centre. It owes its early growth to its position at the junction of a north–south trade route with another one from Thuringia to the lower Rhine. Its importance increased when it became the capital and seat of government for the Electorate of Hesse. Many Huguenots fled here during the seventeenth and eighteenth centuries, and their enterprise, and the advent of the railway, contributed to its industrial development. It is now a centre of the food, chemical and machine industries and houses a Volkswagen branch factory.

Of the other towns only a few can be mentioned. Giessen, located in a good nodal position, is a university town of some industrial importance; while in the northern part of the region is Göttingen, particularly renowned for its science faculty. The northernmost of the towns is Hamlin, a Weser bridge town on the route from Cologne to North-east Germany, and today a centre of flour-milling, but best known in Britain through Browning's version of the legend of the Pied Piper.

Except for the southernmost part, the region belongs to the drainage basin of the Weser and is drained by its headwaters, the Fulda, and the lower part of the Werra, and in the northern section by the Leine and the Weser itself. Navigation on the Weser which was recently improved, begins in fact at Kassel on the Fulda. The winding course of the Weser is as unsuited to land traffic as the Moselle Valley and the main roads and railway follow the straight rift valley of the Leine.

Of the Harz Mountains, only the western part lies in West Germany and thus belongs to this region. Settlement advanced to the heights of the Harz largely because of the silver and other ores, and from the tenth century onwards the Harz became a centre of mining and metallurgy. There is still some mining today, though it is relatively unimportant. Much more significant in the modern landscape is the legacy of abandoned shafts, mill-ponds for the old water-mills, and mining towns and villages. The tradition lives on in a college of mining and a mining museum at Clausthal-Zellerfeld.

The Wasserkuppe, the highest part of the Rhön Mountains, was the cradle of glider flying in Germany.

The Lahn river at Limburg with its famous Romanesque cathedral.

(*Top left*)

Among the smaller towns of the Hesse hill country Marburg is particularly attractive. Its life is so much dominated by its university, the earliest Protestant one in Germany, that it has been said that while other places may have a university, Marburg is a university.

(*Top right*)

Like all the old towns in the hill country of Hesse and the Weser, Hamlin is full of attractive old buildings such as these two burghers' houses.

The Eder, a tributary of the Fulda river, has been dammed and the Eder lake which resulted is the third largest of German reservoirs. Its main purpose is to regulate the flow of the Weser so that shipping can continue during times of drought.

In the Harz the decline of mining did not give rise to large-scale cottage industries as elsewhere in the Uplands, since miners from the Harz were so expert that they always found a welcome in other mining areas. On the whole agriculture, supplemented during the last few decades by the tourist trade, has proved to be a sufficiently broad economic base. There are, however, some specialised occupations like wood-carving. The wood-carver shown here is just putting the finishing touches to the model of a Harz miner in his traditional clothes.

The Weser Valley, which winds through hill country, is not followed by major lines of communication and the Weser itself frequently suffers from low water. Navigation has been much improved after completion of a canalisation scheme in 1960.

The Harz is surrounded by many old towns like Osterode, shown here, which during the Middle Ages profited from the nearby mining and the fact that trade routes followed the edge of the mountains in the north and south. By-passed by the Industrial Revolution, they preserved their medieval features and are now popular with tourists.

8. The South German Scarp and Vale Country

Politically this region consists of most of the Land Baden-Württemberg, the southern parts of the Länder Rhineland-Palatinate and Hesse, Bavaria north of the Danube and the Saarland.

Major cities (in thousands) arranged according to number of inhabitants in 1939:

	1939	1968
Frankfurt-on-Main	553·5	660·8
Stuttgart	458·4	615·0
Nuremberg (*Nürnberg*)	423·4	466·7
Mannheim	285·0	324·3
Karlsruhe	190·1	254·0
Wiesbaden	170·4	258·6
Mainz	158·5	168·9
Ludwigshafen	144·4	173·0
Saarbrücken	133·4	132·6
Darmstadt	115·2	139·5
Freiburg	110·1	161·4
Würzburg	107·5	120·0
Heidelberg	86·5	122·0
Offenbach	85·1	117·0
Fürth	82·3	94·4
Pforzheim	79·6	88·0
Heilbronn	77·6	96·1
Kaiserslautern	70·7	99·7
Esslingen	49·4	82·3
Erlangen	36·0	83·0

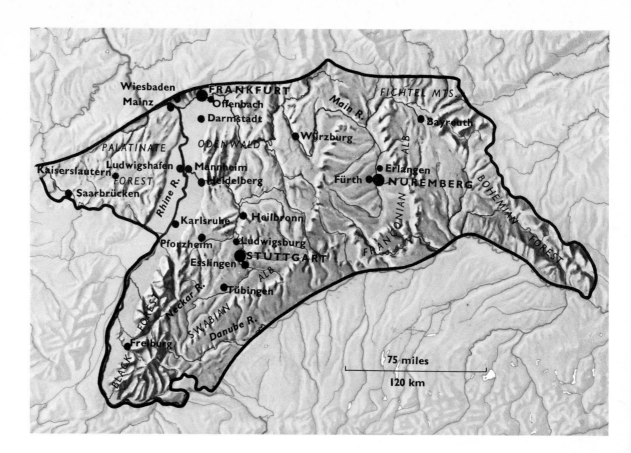

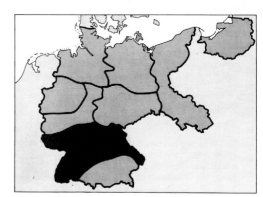

The Uplands drop steeply along a series of faults down to the Rhine plain of the Rift Valley. This is a view from the Haardt, the range of hills on the eastern border of the Pfalz (Palatinate), but the view is very much the same from anywhere along the fault scarp. Note the narrow strip fields of this intensively farmed fertile stretch.

The vineyards of the Rhine Rift Valley are less spectacular than those of the Rhine Gorge but produce nearly three-quarters of all German wine. The average total wine harvest of Germany is about 300 million litres per year. A view of Oppenheim, the centre of an important vine-growing district south of Mainz.

This region stretches from the flood plain of the Rhine Rift Valley and the Franco-German border to the heights of the Bohemian Forest, and from the Rhön Mountains to the plateau of the Swabian Alb. What unites this great diversity of landscapes is the fact that, rather like a honeycomb, the whole area consists of fertile basins surrounded by ranges of hills which connect each one to, and yet isolates it from its neighbours.

The most obvious contrast is between basins and hill ranges, but there are many others. The character of the hills differs greatly according to the rock of which they are formed. Gneiss and granite in the highest parts, the Black Forest and the Bohemian Forest, give rise to well-rounded ridges, large areas of which are still covered with woodland. The landscape is similar where the hills are formed of Bunter sandstone, as in the Palatinate Forest. The permeable limestone is responsible for the pronounced scarps of the Swabian and Franconian Alb where most of the forest was cleared as early as prehistoric times, since the lime-rich soils were particularly suited to primitive agriculture.

This differentiation between early settled areas and areas into which settlement expanded from the sixth century onwards, and the close juxtaposition of these contrasting areas, is another regional characteristic. Consequently settlement is greatly diversified. Large, irregular, nucleated villages are found in the early settled and fertile areas, while hamlets or isolated farms are typical of the late-settled poorer soils. Equally great is the contrast between the large modern cities and small market towns, preserved with all their medieval features in greater numbers here than anywhere else in Germany. Moreover, nowhere else in Germany are there so many small towns, no more than villages in size; this is a result of the intense political fragmentation which characterised South-west Germany during the Middle Ages.

Except for the Saar coalfield this region is relatively poor in natural resources, though iron ore, salt and oil are produced. There are nevertheless a few highly industrialised areas which came into being either because of the easy communications offered by the Rhine, Main or Neckar rivers, or from a combination of rural over-population (where small farms predominate) with a good deal of traditional skill. In the former case the result was factory industry, in the latter mainly semi-rural, cottage-type industry, such as watch- and clock-making.

In the Rhineland, the meeting-place of Roman and Teuton civilisation, German culture reached its earliest heights. Witness to this are the many ancient buildings, like the Romanesque cathedral at Worms, the city of the Nibelungen legend. Worms is also of historical fame for the Diet of 1521 to which Martin Luther was summoned to retract his writings. This he refused to do, concluding with the proud words, "Here I stand, I cannot do otherwise, so help me God, Amen."

Badly blitzed Frankfurt has now a completely new face, though the most important ancient features are still left as a reminder of its great past, like this, the last of the towers on the city wall. A reflection of its present importance is that it is the "financial capital" of West Germany and Frankfurt airport, with over 6 million passengers in 1967, is the busiest on the Continent, but still well behind London's Heathrow with 12·7 million passengers in the same year.

The German Upper Rhine Valley and the Main and Neckar Basins

These three sub-regions have much in common. Favoured by climate and fertile loess soils they are among the best agricultural areas of Germany and support the most exacting crops. Vineyards reach high up the slopes, interspersed with orchards, which include such delicate trees as peach, apricot and almond, while the level stretches are covered with wheat and sugar-beet fields and plantations of hops and tobacco. Settlements lie close together and many villages have the appearance of small towns. Only the flood plains are devoid of settlement and along the Rhine, which was regulated and confined into an artificial bed during the later nineteenth century, there are extensive pine forests.

All three rivers have been made navigable, the Main and Neckar by the building of a number of barrages with locks. This has greatly facilitated the process of industrialisation in these valleys.

The largest and most important industrial district has developed at the junction of the Rhine and the Main and consists of such old towns as Frankfurt and Mainz as well as towns that grew out of villages, such as Rüsselsheim, one of the oldest and most important motor car manufacturing towns. Vehicle building and electrical engineering are the most important industries, but this area is also well known for its jewellery and leather goods.

Frankfurt (the ford of the Franks) is the metropolis of this industrial zone. Strategically placed for communications, it became an important medieval trade centre and fair town. It rose to the rank of Free Imperial City, a city not subject to any ruler except the Emperor, and became the place where the German Emperor was elected and crowned. Industrial growth almost inevitably followed its emergence as a railway junction and though its industry is extremely varied, its chemical plant (dye works at Höchst) is the most noteworthy. A recent development, following the division of Germany, is that Frankfurt has become the "capital" of the fur trade, formerly concentrated at Leipzig.

Publishing, too, whose home before 1945 was Leipzig, has migrated to this area, but to another city, Wiesbaden. This city, in the first instance a spa (as its name *-baden* indicates), has hot mineral springs which attract some 100,000 visitors every year. In addition Wiesbaden has become the capital of Hesse with important administrative functions.

Opposite Wiesbaden, on the left bank of the Rhine, lies Mainz. It has a long history—its name is derived from the Roman castle *Moguntiacum* which it replaced; in 748 it became the see of the first German archbishopric, initially held by the Anglo-Saxon missionary, Wynfrith Boniface, the apostle of the Germans. In later years it became the home of the inventor of printing, Gutenberg, and therefore of those practising this revolutionary technique. Today Mainz is of industrial importance, a major Rhine port, capital of the Land Rhineland-Palatinate and seat of the first post-war German university.

The southern apex of the Rhine–Main industrial triangle is formed by Darmstadt, whose chemical and pharmaceutical industry has largely been responsible for the recent growth of the town which also has a university specialising in technology.

Only about 50 kilometres to the south lies the second major industrial centre, the twin city of Mannheim and Ludwigshafen. Mannheim, the older of the two, founded in the early seventeenth century, is a relative newcomer in this region of ancient cities, but Ludwigshafen, dating from 1843, is even more recent. Owing its spectacular growth to the Industrial Revolution, it now boasts a giant chemical plant (BASF) and specialises in the production of agricultural machinery, electrical engineering and shipbuilding.

Not far away, at the point where the Neckar river enters the Rhine plain, lies the picturesque city of Heidelberg, famous for its university, the oldest in Germany, founded in 1386. Of international repute, it further resembles Oxford in that its outskirts towards the Rhine have become increasingly industrialised.

Situated, like Heidelberg, some distance from the Rhine are two more large cities, Karlsruhe and Freiburg. Both have important industries, but neither is the centre of an industrial concentration. Karlsruhe is a foundation of the early eighteenth century. Of particular interest is its ground-plan; all main streets radiate from the centre, the site of the former palace of the Grand Duke.

The Frankfurt Trade Fair dating back to the thirteenth century has the longest tradition of all German fairs and is still of great importance.

Christmas at the Wiesbaden Kurhaus—the place where one takes the waters.

The old part of Heidelberg, hemmed in between the castle hill and the river, is very densely built up and its narrow, winding streets present a serious traffic problem. Expansion of the city and the university has therefore been taking place to the west on a section of the so-called "Bergstrasse". This is a zone of loess-covered land—very fertile and intensively cultivated—which stretches along the foot of the eastern fault scarp. Not surprisingly, this expansion has resulted in some friction between town and country.

The south gate of the reconstructed Saalburg north of Frankfurt, one of the many castles along the Roman Wall or "Limes". The line it follows from north of Koblenz to Ratisbon is of importance for the human geography of Germany since it divides the country into one part where urban civilisation is based on Roman tradition and another part where city life is of medieval origin.

Hanau, near Frankfurt, is famous for its jewellery made in workshops like this. Similarly specialised is nearby Offenbach where high-quality leather goods are produced and where an international leather goods fair is held at the same time as the Frankfurt Fair.

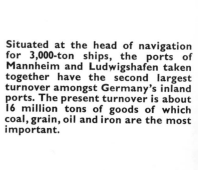

Situated at the head of navigation for 3,000-ton ships, the ports of Mannheim and Ludwigshafen taken together have the second largest turnover amongst Germany's inland ports. The present turnover is about 16 million tons of goods of which coal, grain, oil and iron are the most important.

Although this city is a latecomer, as the ducal residence and later the railway terminus of the former Grand Duchy, it achieved its present status with little difficulty. Freiburg, founded in the twelfth century, is much older. An important market, especially for wine and for timber from the Black Forest, it is also a university city.

In the Main Valley itself, except for the Frankfurt region, there are no industrial centres comparable in size to those already mentioned. Of its cities only one, the bishop's city of Würzburg, with its impressive medieval castle, is of comparable size. It was so badly damaged in an air raid that it was seriously suggested that the ruins be left as a permanent reminder of the tragedy of war, and a new Würzburg be built near by; in the end it was rebuilt on the original site and the number of inhabitants, which had sunk to a few thousand, has risen beyond expectations. It plays a significant part in the Franconian wine trade, and is also a university city with some industry.

The largest and most important urban concentration of the Main basin, the city of Nuremberg, lies on a southern tributary of the Main. Founded about A.D. 1000, Nuremberg became a medieval Mecca for trade and craftsmen, a centre of invention (watches, drawn wire), of learning (Behaim globe) and of the arts (Mastersingers, Albrecht Dürer). Modern industrialisation began early, since it was here, through the enterprise of its citizens, that the first German railway, using a Stephenson engine and an English driver, was built in 1835 to link it with Fürth, now part of the

The house of Albrecht Dürer, one of the greatest German artists and the most famous burgher of Nuremberg, has been carefully restored after war damage.

The Gothic cathedral of Freiburg is justly famous, but to see it covered in snow like this is relatively rare.

The bishop's palace at Würzburg, a Baroque masterpiece, is a particular jewel of this ancient city.

Nuremberg is famous for its toys and an international toy trade fair is held there annually.

On stage—a scene from *Parsifal*.

Off stage—during an interval.

Of all international music festivals the Wagner festivals at Bayreuth have the longest tradition.

The birthplace of the poet and pl wright, Friedrich Schiller, in the lit town of Marbach, near Stuttgart.

Nuremberg conurbation. Most important for its economy are now the various branches of electrical engineering, especially if one also includes within the conurbation Erlangen, where the giant Siemens concern established its headquarters after 1945, resulting in a doubling in size of this formerly quiet university town.

In the Neckar basin Nuremberg finds, at least in some respects, a parallel in Stuttgart, the former capital of Württemberg, and present capital of the new Land Baden-Württemberg. Surrounded by vineyards, it has remained one of the most beautiful German cities in spite of being the core of Württemberg's industry. Lacking local raw material, its industries have developed through the use of extremely skilled labour, and the products of Stuttgart and Württemberg have, for quality, no rival in the world. Out of the great number of products of this industrial region, which covers almost the entire southern Neckar basin without however giving rise to an industrial landscape in the usual sense, watches and clocks, precision instruments, electrical goods, accordions and jewellery are the most outstanding. These and its motor cars are

all products of "growth industries" that have expanded particularly rapidly and attracted workers, including many from abroad.

The Saarland

Of the local industrial districts one deserves special mention, the Saarland. It is untypical partly because the prevailing industry is heavy industry based on the Saar coalfield and partly for political reasons. France, to whom an additional source of coking coal would be extremely welcome, tried after both the First and the Second World Wars to appropriate the Saarland from Germany. The people of the Saar have each time, however, shown unmistakably that they wish to remain part of Germany. France has wisely acquiesced, an action which has removed a major obstacle to good relations between these two countries.

Before large-scale coal-mining began there around 1850 the Saarland was of little economic importance, though it had had some ironworks since 1600. It is a hill country with poor soils and was widely covered with forests; even today woodlands cover a

Stuttgart is situated in a basin off the main natural routeway and surrounded by hills, so that all rail routes have to use tunnels to get there. However, as the capital of Württemberg, it was able to outgrow better sited towns near by and become the largest city in South-west Germany.

third of the country. Geologically it is a basin formed by the coal measures, so that mining spread in the deep and wide Saar Valley and its northern branch valleys where coal comes nearest to the surface. Although it is not very good coking coal, the nearby Lorraine iron-ore field boosted the development of coal-mining to supply coke for the blast-furnaces in the Saarland itself and also in Lorraine to which it became linked by a canal over a century ago. A special feature of the Saarland came to be the particularly large number of miners and industrial workers who were also smallholders. This was an advantage during times of economic recessions and food shortages, but during the post-war industrial boom it resulted in much land being left uncultivated.

The Daimler-Benz plant, the oldest automobile factory in the world and makers of Mercedes cars as well as Porsche (also at Stuttgart), make prestige cars which have been described as superb pieces of machinery put together with all the skill and loving thoroughness that German engineers can command.

The vineyards on the slopes of the Neckar near Stuttgart produce an excellent wine but, since most of it is consumed locally, it is not widely known abroad.

81

Tübingen on the Neckar with its university, founded in 1477, has a cultural importance in Württemberg disproportionate to its size; about 17 per cent of its inhabitants are students.

Over a third of the steel production of the Saarland is concentrated at Völklingen. The iron and steel works which had been in the hands of the Röchling family for generations were sequestrated by the French administration in 1945, but were returned at the unanimous desire of the Saarlanders.

Farmhouses in Württemberg. Most of the farms are small or medium size and mechanisation is only advancing slowly. Even cows are often used as draft animals, thus greatly reducing their milk yield. The wealth of a farmer is judged by the size of his midden.

The Wooded Uplands

Many parts of the German Uplands are called *Wald* (forest), but it would be wrong to imagine them as continuous forests. These are historical names dating back to the time when the Uplands really were covered by woodlands, but from the sixth century onwards all these forests have been penetrated by settlers and allowed to remain therefore only on the most unfavourable soils. In the Black Forest, Spessart, and the German share of the Bohemian Forest, heavily wooded though they are, forests cover only about half of the area. Nevertheless, farming in these parts is quite different from that of the lowlands, resembling more closely that of the Alpine valleys. Arable cultivation is carried out as ley farming and is of little importance; emphasis is placed on cattle-rearing. Meadows and pastures occupy the largest proportion of the cleared stretches and there are even some summer pastures at the highest altitudes, though, unlike those in the Alps, these have been artificially cleared.

The forest plays an important role in the life of the farmer. Every farmer owns some woodland and this is his savings box to which he can turn in an emergency. The woods also provide opportunities for additional employment, and most people are in one way or another dependent on income from the forest. Wood-cutting, transporting the logs, sawmills and the making of wooden implements, churns and a host of other things play their part. Best known of the Black Forest products are the wooden cuckoo clocks. This industry began in the seventeenth century as a purely peasant occupation. It was only during the nineteenth century that clock-making, and then watch-making as well, came to be carried out in workshops and eventually factories.

In the Bohemian Forest the development from peasant industry to factory industry led to specialisation in furniture-making and also glass-making, based on quartz sand as well as wood. The latter was important for two reasons: as ash supplying the potassium, the second major constituent of glass, and as fuel.

Timber utilisation inevitably affected the composition of the forests. Originally the slopes were covered up to about 1,000 metres by beechwoods and it was only higher up that the woods consisted of conifers, mainly spruce. Now spruce plantations cover wide areas at lower altitudes too, since in replanting the more quickly maturing conifers are preferred to broadleaf trees.

Both the Bohemian Forest and to a greater degree the Black Forest have attracted increasing numbers of tourists in summer as well as for winter sports. The Black Forest was in fact one of the areas where ski-ing was pioneered on the Continent after its introduction from Norway towards the end of the nineteenth century.

A small valley in the Black Forest. Isolated farms are the most usual form of settlement in upland areas cleared during the later Middle Ages.

The hill country of the Palatinate is a chequerboard of wooded heights and clearings with narrow field strips, the result of the custom of divided inheritance.

Dark fir woods stretch for miles on the heights of the Bohemian Forest. Note the boulder field in the foreground.

9. The German Alps and their Foreland

Politically this region includes Bavaria south of the Danube and the south-eastern part of Baden-Württemberg.

Major cities (in thousands) arranged according to number of inhabitants in 1939:

	1939	1968
Munich (*München*)	829·3	1260·6
Augsburg	184·4	210·6
Ratisbon (*Regensburg*)	95·6	125·1
Ulm (including Neu-Ulm)	89·0	115·3
Ingolstadt	33·4	69·4

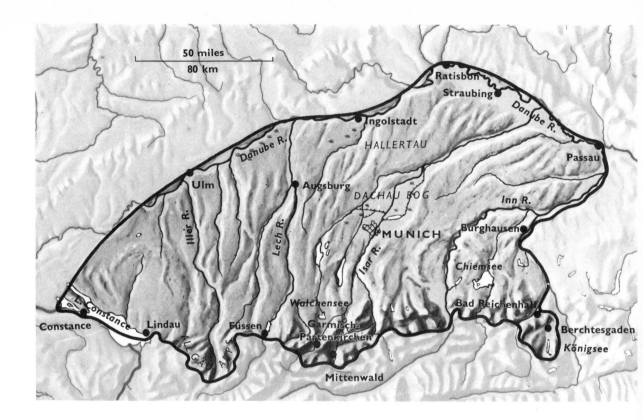

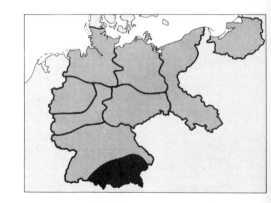

84

Despite their apparent dissimilarity, the lofty peaks of the German Alps and their Foreland together form an important geographical unit. In the first place, they have a common geomorphic origin. As the Alps rose, the Foreland subsided, and the resulting trough was filled by waste material deposited by the Alpine streams. The Alpine glaciers of the Ice Age both brought down more debris to form morainic hills, and also excavated basins. Their melt-waters spread the glacial drift and deposited it as gravel-sheets and terraces. The wind blowing down the Alpine glaciers picked up fine dust particles and dropped them some distance away to form the fertile loess cover of the northern Foreland. Climatically, the Alps affect the Foreland by causing the north-westerly winds to rise so that precipitation is increased there.

There is evidence in human geography too of regional similarities. Settlement advanced into the Alps from the Foreland so that we find the same kind of peoples north and south of the mountains' edge; in the Alps, as in the Foreland, there are people speaking Bavarian dialects east of the Lech river and those speaking Swabian dialects west of it. The passes and valleys which guide the lines of communication across the Alps extend their influence into the Foreland. Towns have developed either at their point of entry into this region, or, farther away where a number of different Alpine routes, converging together on a west–east routeway, branch out again into separate routeways to the north.

The Alpine Foreland

Like the West Rhenish provinces and the German south-west, the Alpine Foreland was also part of the Roman Empire, and it is not surprising that the Romans were the first to build roads through the Alpine passes and also towns to serve as fortresses and trade centres. Some of the modern towns betray their Roman origin in name as well as location. Augsburg, for instance, has developed from the leading Roman town in this region, *Augusta Vindelicorum*; during the Middle Ages and after it was not only the focal point of the Alpine Foreland but was amongst the most important centres of trade and craftsmanship in the whole of Middle Europe. The houses of the wealthy merchants are still witnesses to this period of glory. Not that Augsburg is unimportant today; the

Both the humble houses in the foreground, built by a wealthy merchant for the poor citizens in the early sixteenth century, and the mighty town hall in the background, bear witness to the early importance and prosperity of the free imperial city of Augsburg.

Munich is a city with many facets, but arts, science, industry and the enjoyment of life are the most important. The Deutsche Museum, on its island site, is a unique museum of science and technology. On the right is shown a marquee during the October festival, a fair which attracts about 6 million visitors.

traditional home of a flourishing textile industry, it has added a metal industry and machine building—indeed, it is famous as the place where Diesel invented his engine.

With the coming of the railways it was, however, superseded by the younger Munich—the name means "place of the monks"—a town not founded until the twelfth century. Situated on the Isar, the Foreland river still most frequently used by timber rafts (there are now about 4,000 to 5,000 a year), Munich occupies a favourable site where the river is neither as deeply incised as farther south, nor lacks protecting banks, as to the north, and where in the past an island made the dangerous crossing easier. In addition, Munich is advantageously placed in the centre of the Alpine Foreland. Nevertheless the fundamental reasons for its growth are historical rather than physical. Important for its early development was the "salt concession" of 1332, a monopoly which made it compulsory for all salt from the saltworks of Reichenhall and elsewhere to cross the Isar at Munich. While Augsburg was a Free Imperial City, Munich remained subject to the Duke of Bavaria and became the capital in 1505. This, although at first a handicap

because it impeded the initiative of the burghers, later proved to be a decisive advantage. In 1806 Bavaria became a kingdom, doubling its area and quadrupling its population, an increase which was reflected in the growth of its capital. With enhanced administrative importance, Munich also became the archbishop's see and a university city. It came to be a home of the arts in Germany, then a centre of science and literature and later the most vital railway junction in South Germany.

This, and the foundation of the Reich in 1871, set it on the path which led to commercial and industrial supremacy in this region. It became the most important distribution point for grain, timber, fruit and vegetables from the south and south-east. Its beer is world-famous, but alongside the brewing industry other branches of manufacture developed such as the motor and optical industries —BMW (Bavarian Motor Works), Agfa camera plant—and electrical engineering. To the latter branch belongs Munich's largest single factory, part of the Siemens concern, with a labour force of over 20,000. In addition it is also a publishing centre and, with its art galleries, festivals and congresses, a pivot of the tourist trade.

The famous Weltenburg monastery, founded in the eighth century, is situated above Ratisbon in the picturesque Danube gorge where the river has had to cut its way through Jurassic limestone.

Where the Danube reaches its northernmost point lies Ratisbon, the successor to the Roman *Castra Regina*. It has many claims to fame, one being its cathedral and its cathedral boys' choir; the "Ratisbon cathedral sparrows".

The final stimulus was the division of Germany in 1945, as a result of which Munich, which has even been termed "the secret capital of Germany", took over a number of Berlin's functions. The Munich studios for instance became the centre of the West German film industry, and Munich University is now the largest in Germany.

The enhanced importance of Munich has been reflected also in its *umland* (surrounding area). A notable example is Ingolstadt. Previously an old fortress town and local market without industry, it was after 1945 chosen as a location for the Auto Union motor works (formerly in Saxony) and then as the terminal of three crude oil pipe-lines (from Marseilles, Genoa and Trieste) and the site of three giant refineries. As oil refining requires large amounts of water Ingolstadt's situation on the Danube has once again become of importance.

During the Middle Ages and later, it was the Danube as a waterway which contributed to the growth of its riverside cities as far upstream as Ulm, which is still considered the head of navigation, although there is virtually none above Ratisbon. Without the river traffic Ulm would never have become one of the leading free imperial cities. Its former wealth can be judged by its famous minster, a Gothic edifice, with the highest church tower in the world. In the case of Ratisbon, navigation was a contributory factor to its growth, which was also a result of its location at a crossing-point of ancient trade routes and its being a bishop's see. Following improvements to the navigation channel shipping is once again important; Ratisbon is Germany's leading Danube port with an annual turnover of about 3 million tons.

The Danube tributaries also served formerly as waterways, and many charming old towns can be found along them too. There is one apparent exception to this general tendency for urban location: Lake Constance, where the towns are on the lake shores. The lake itself, bordered by and shared amongst Germany, Switzerland and Austria, is the feature which most noticeably sets this region apart from the rest of the Alpine Foreland. This mighty body of water, jokingly referred to as the "Swabian Sea", not only enables the Rhine to deposit its debris and to even out the irregularities of its flow—an important consideration for the Rhine's suitability as a waterway—but even influences the climate along the lake shores. These are covered by vineyards and orchards and settlement is of great antiquity.

At low water, remains of Neolithic and Bronze Age pile dwellings can still be seen and many places are of Roman foundation. Constance, a bishop's and former Free Imperial City, was handicapped in its later development by its bridgehead situation on the southern, i.e. Swiss, shore; this deprived it of an immediate hinterland. It has nevertheless remained the most important city on the shores of the lake, and has many old buildings including the mansion where the Council of 1414–18 was held; it is also a great tourist attraction. Its new university aims to be a small élite institution.

The Lake Constance region is a special case within the zone of moraines. This lies between the Alps and the belt of terminal moraines, which as a series of crescents, convex towards the north, forms the northern boundary of the region. The physical features of this zone are a widespread cover of glacial debris known as ground moraine, small hills of glacial origin called drumlins, and lakes or peat bogs which now lie in the paths of the former glaciers. The lakes, whose changing colours enhance the chequerboard of the meadows, pastures and woods among which they lie, are a particular attraction to visitors. Apart from Lake Constance the lakes in the western part of this region are numerous but small, while in the east they are fewer in number, but larger. The farmsteads frequently stand on their own and you will often see chapels or village churches with the onion-shaped steeples so typical of South Germany.

The moraines of the earlier glaciations farther to the north have largely lost their hilly character and with less rain and soil of loess or loam the grassland gives way to arable farming.

The zone of moraines ends abruptly, giving way to the zone of gravel-sheets. In itself, this area is divided into an eastern part where the outwash material of all glaciations lies one layer on another, and a western part where it is deposited in the form of terraces. The eastern gravel-sheet, also called the "inclined plain of Munich", is in its southern part largely covered by extensive forests of pine and firs, almost the only form of land-use possible on this poor and permeable soil. The thickness of the gravel-sheet

The ancient bishop's city of Passau, successor to the Roman *Castra Batava*, at the confluence of the Inn (left) and the Danube (right). On the Inn, once also an important waterway, navigation ceased in the nineteenth century owing to the swiftness of its current and great variations in its flow.

A reconstructed Bronze Age hamlet at Unter-Uhldingen shows the advanced culture existing in this region 3,000 years ago. In the background is Birnau monastery, a Baroque building that blends harmoniously with the landscape.

decreases northwards and by approximately the latitude of Munich it has become so thin that the ground-water comes to the surface; north of Munich there are therefore extensive bogs, now partly reclaimed, partly used for peat cutting. One of the largest is the Dachau Bog, a name which most people connect with the notorious Nazi concentration camp built there.

In the western part only the "low terrace" is covered by woods and heath and is as inimical to settlement as the entire eastern gravel-sheet; the loess layer of the "high terrace" favours arable farming. Archaeological finds and the prevailing place-names are proof that this area has been settled for a long time. In the southern parts most people live in hamlets, while large, nucleated, irregular villages with open fields predominate in the north.

An area of Tertiary hills forms the north-eastern section of the Alpine Foreland. The humid valleys of these are mainly meadow-land, but the higher parts with a thick loess and loam cover are intensively farmed with wheat and, in a limited area north of Munich, the Hallertau, with hops.

Another very fertile part of the Tertiary hills area is the Dungau, Bavaria's "grain chest". Here wheat and stall-fed cattle are the mainstays of farming. The market for the products is the old and picturesque city of Straubing.

Not far from Munich is the Hallertau district where the rectangular-shaped hop fields give the landscape its characteristic note.

The art enthusiast is drawn by the great number of beautiful Baroque churches in southern Bavaria. Shown here is the choir of the Wies Kirche (church in the meadow), one of the most famous.

A view near Bad Reichenhall. To allow the grass to dry more thoroughly it is heaped on to wooden stilts—these are popularly known as "little hay men". Another method often used is hanging the grass on temporary wires.

Farms at a small glacial lake near Mittenwald. Although there are some villages, most of the farmhouses in the Alps are isolated or in small groups. Characteristic of the Bavarian farmhouse is the fact that man and beast live under the same roof—a gently sloping roof, covered by wooden shingles and weighed down by boulders. The smaller house with each farm serves as a dwelling for the old farmer after he has handed the holding over to a son; when not used for this it may be let to summer visitors.

A view of the city of Lindau on its island site. Opposite the city is the point where the Rhine enters the lake (it leaves it again at Constance). Lindau lies very close to the boundary of Germany; the eastern shore of the lake (on the left) is Austrian territory, and the mountains in the background to the south are in Switzerland.

This shows the Hall of Mirrors in the royal chateau of Herrenchiemsee which, situated on an island of the Chiemsee, with the Alps in the background, has a finer setting than Versailles, on which it was modelled.

In the economy of the Alps timber is pre-eminent. While most of the wood is used for conventional purposes such as building, paper-making and heating, some places are famous for particular highly skilled crafts, such as wood-carving, or as here at Mittenwald, violin-making.

It often takes some hours to reach the summer pastures from the home farm, but it is not often that a lake has to be crossed as well, as has to be done by some farmers living on the shores of the Königsee.

The Alps

While Germany's industrial regions attract people for employment, the Alps exert their pull over the country and beyond as an area of rest and enjoyment. Only a small part of the Alps are within Germany, but this makes their importance to the nation proportionately greater. We need no reminder of the refreshment and relaxation which they offer, winter and summer, to thousands of people. Almost all the towns, villages and hamlets and even isolated country inns cater at some level for German and foreign visitors, and this "second harvest" has been very important in an area where farming is largely at subsistence level and where there are few other means of employment. Of no less significance are the indirect consequences of tourism, such as the improvement of communication lines to formerly out-of-the-way places, and the stimulus given to the building trade.

Tourism is, however, a recent development in the Alps. It has, in fact, succeeded the custom of spa-visiting and there are still a number of these resorts based on iodine or brine springs or specialising in mud cures. Earlier still came pilgrimages to shrines which, quite apart from their religious associations, now attract visitors with architectural interests. Often equally rewarding are the many other churches, monasteries, castles and chateaux, as well as a great number of more modest buildings.

Unique in Germany are the life and work of the peasants whose ancestors cleared the forest and built permanent settlements at over 1,000 metres. Although some grain is grown at this altitude (and under conditions which would make a lowland farmer blench, since often no machinery whatsoever can be used), the Alps are a region of cattle-farming in so far as farming is possible at all. The meadows around the farm provide hay for winter feed, while the livestock grazes during the summer months on the natural Alpine grassland above the mantle of forest. So vital is it to provide sufficient winter feed that on slopes too steep for pasture the grass is cut by harvesters secured by ropes and wearing crampons for safety.

Economically forestry is much more important than farming. The forest which covers nearly half the area of the German Alps largely determines the character of the landscape on the middle and lower slopes, and the livelihoods of many people. There is first the forester; he not only tends the forest but also looks after the game, of which the most notable are the roe and red deer and at greater altitudes, the shy chamois. Then there are the gay wood-cutters whose work under Alpine conditions is particularly strenuous and dangerous. Since clear cutting of larger areas increases the likelihood of landslides and avalanches, most of the cutting is selective, making the task more difficult still. Transporting the roughly dressed logs down to the roads is mostly done in winter by hand sledges, again a perilous undertaking. Finally there are those who work the timber in sawmills or make wooden implements, as well as the particularly gifted wood-carvers or violin-makers.

There is one last role which the Alps play in Germany: they are the most important single source of hydroelectricity. Of all electricity produced in West Germany, hydroelectricity accounts for only about a tenth, but most of this is generated in the power stations at the foot of the Alps. It should be added that Germany also imports large quantities of electricity from the Austrian Alps, which are linked by direct transmission lines with the Ruhr region where consumption is particularly high.

The best known of Germany's large hydro power stations is the combined Walchensee-Kochelsee plant, situated north-west of Garmisch-Partenkirchen, which makes use of two natural lakes, one lying about 200 metres below the other. To increase the effectiveness of the plant, the catchment area has been artificially increased by tapping the Isar and also by diverting a stream which used to flow southward to join the Inn river.

Most of the farmland in the Alps and their immediate foreland is devoted to hay production and supports the cattle and dairy farming for which the upper Lech region, the Allgäu, is particularly famous.

The settlements in the German Alps are particularly rich in folklore; the Maypole, often beautifully decorated, is a common sight, and traditional costumes are widely worn, especially in the Berchtesgaden region.

The salt resources of the Bavarian Alps have been for various reasons a constant attraction since prehistoric times. At Bad Reichenhall the natural brine is still used in a number of ways for curing ailments; thousands of people annually visit the salt mines at Berchtesgaden. Shown here is a party in miner's clothing at the end of such a trip.

Füssen, situated on the Lech river at the German-Austrian boundary, has town walls and old churches which are a great tourist attraction. Note the barrage in the foreground which helps in flood control and also facilitates the generation of electricity.

From the top of the Wank mountain above Garmisch-Partenkirchen, easily reached by a cable railway of which a number were built in the inter-war period and several more after 1945, there is a unique view of the highest mountain of Germany, the Zugspitze (2,964 metres). This is climbed by a cog and pinion railway. Note the numerous hay barns dotted over the cleared land.

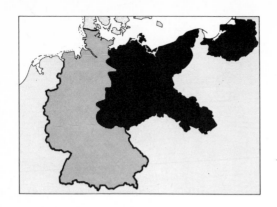

10. Germany east of the Elbe-Saale line

A belt of land stretching almost due south from around Lübeck to the Fichtel Mountains is an important geographical divide of very long standing. Named the Elbe–Saale line, after the two main rivers which flow through it, its major significance lies within the sphere of human geography. Its first emergence as a cultural geographical boundary took place over a thousand years ago when the Teutonic tribes, which were eventually to form the German people, settled down more permanently after the period of wandering which led to the downfall of the Roman Empire (see maps on page 12). It thus became the area where German and Slav settlement met. Civilisation developed rapidly in the German lands as a result of the marriage of Latin culture and Teutonic vigour; the first towns came into being and an advanced type of agriculture, using a heavy plough with an iron ploughshare, led to an expansion of farmland on to the heavy soils and much clearing of woodland. Development in the Slav lands to the east was much slower. By about A.D. 1000 onwards, when the German settlers moved eastwards, in many cases invited by the native Slav rulers to bring the benefits of this advanced civilisation to their countries, the contrasting geographical features of the German and Slav lands were already firmly established. Although during the next three centuries these former Slav lands also became German, undergoing a similar expansion of farmland and a development of towns, the contrasts between "East and West Elbia" remained. While in the West the opening up of the interior had been a process gradually advancing by trial and error, in the East it was, almost from the beginning, a large-scale and planned undertaking applying the lessons learnt in the old homeland. Development in the East was directed by *locatores*, settlement contractors one might call them, who were not only responsible for recruiting the settlers and taking them to their new domiciles, but also for laying out the ground-plans of fields, villages and towns. It is thus not surprising that despite their great number the settlements can be grouped into a few types, all of which have one thing in common: an extremely regular layout, something which in West Elbia is the exception rather than the rule.

While the medieval towns in the West mostly have an irregular ground-plan and winding streets, the characteristic ground-plan of the old towns in the East is an oval wall surrounding a grid-iron pattern of streets with a large market square in the centre. In the West the typical rural settlement is the large nucleated village of irregular layout, with a complicated system of open fields. In the East one finds, however, the "street village", the "green village" and the "round village", and villages with an elongated ground-plan such as the "forest village" and the "marsh village". The land of the first three types is arranged in very regular open fields, while in the last two the entire land of each farm is in a single plot.

As these villages were laid out, one holding, much larger than the others and also endowed with special privileges, was always set aside as a reward for the *locator*. This led subsequently to a

Patschkau (Paczków) in Upper Silesia, with its regular layout, is a typical example of what most towns in Middle and East Germany used to be like. Although this is a pre-war photograph, the author has seen that the townscape has not changed at all.

The type of village most frequently found on the plains of Middle and East Germany is the Strassendorf (street village), like this one in Lower Silesia.

Typical of the settlement in the Sudeten Mountains are the Waldhufendörfer (forest villages) like this where the land of each farm stretches from the road up the slope in a long strip. The boulders from the fields were collected along the boundaries, and over the centuries gave rise to rough stone walls.

Characteristic of the eighteenth-century development are villages like this in Upper Silesia which, in their extreme regularity, are a vivid expression of the period of Absolutism in which they were founded. Villages of this type are much more frequent in East Elbia, further emphasising the contrast between the old Volksland and the areas of expansion to the East.

further differentiation between West and East Elbia, since these holdings were the nuclei from which developed, mainly after the Thirty Years War, the large farms and estates of the country squires, the *Junker*. This caused the difference in human geography between the old homeland and the eastern territories to become even more marked.

Urban growth during the later nineteenth and twentieth centuries tended to blur the distinction between West and East in the large towns and cities. The basic contrast between the rural pattern in West and East remained, though after 1918 a few estates were divided into smaller holdings or new holdings were created on land surrendered voluntarily from large estates.

Lately this contrast between West and East Elbia has become re-emphasised as a result of the political division of Germany, since the boundary which separates the West German State and the G.D.R. runs north of Magdeburg within this border zone. To the south the boundary between these two political units lies farther to the west so that Thuringia, a part of the original German homeland, now lies east of it. Although Thuringia does not therefore truly belong to the areas of medieval expansion, it is included with them for two reasons. First, in the inter-war period Thuringia became an integral part of a closely knit economic region which developed around the industrial core of Saxony; secondly, within "East Germany" as a whole many political and economic measures have been carried out which have had striking geographical results, and these, too, have linked Thuringia more closely to the regions to the east of it. Amongst these measures were: the expropriation of all farms and estates larger than 100 hectares and their splitting up into small and medium-sized holdings—in so far as they were not taken over as State farms; the establishment on the Soviet pattern of about 600 machine and tractor stations to promote mechanisation of farming and collectivisation of agriculture and the drive to establish such collective farms. These collective farms (called "agricultural production associations"), together with the State farms, covered by the middle of 1959 nearly half of the total farmland, and by April 1960 there was hardly a private farmholding left. As a result the former field boundaries are becoming obliterated and, in adjusting to this different kind of farming, farmhouses and villages have been changing their appearance. In particular the collective farms—of the type where not only the arable land but machinery and livestock too are pooled, the so-called type III—needed large new cowsheds, barns and various other outbuildings. Where new dwelling-houses for members of the collective have been and are being built, they are no longer farmhouses but resemble small suburban houses; even large blocks of flats in villages are now a common sight. This process of change varies regionally and, though slow up till now, it is gaining momentum as building material is becoming more easily available.

Estate farms, like this near Breslau (Wroclaw), used to be a frequent sight in the regions east of the Elbe–Saale line.

A former estate farm in Silesia which, in the inter-war period, was divided up into smaller farms, on a voluntary basis.

Eastward expansion of the German settlers did not halt at the Oder and Neisse rivers, but went much farther into areas now parts of Poland and the Soviet Union. These areas, as far as they were part of the German Reich within its boundaries of 1937, and Danzig (Gdańsk), have been included in this book as its final chapter. Some geographers and readers will think this unjustified owing to the many changes that have taken place. That there have been important changes nobody can deny, and since they are different from those within the G.D.R., it is equally certain that the Oder–Neisse line is an important geographical boundary.

Following the change in political control, the most important change was the expulsion of most of the remaining German population and its replacement by Polish people, mainly from the areas that Poland had to cede to the Soviet Union. However, there are regional differences and thus variations in the degree of subsequent landscape changes. Where a large proportion of the original population is still present, as in the rural areas of Upper Silesia, the changes are hardly noticeable. In the other parts some collective farms were established, but the main difference to the traditional German landscape is that many farms are in a neglected state and war-damaged buildings are still numerous. In the case of towns the situation is similar. Even compared with Middle Germany the making good of war damage lags far behind; in fact more buildings have become ruins merely through neglect. It must, however, also be pointed out that, mainly in the more important towns, damaged historic buildings have been carefully restored and this process will certainly continue. Lately there has also been some building of blocks of flats. Dating from the post-Stalin period they are built in a simple functional style, quite similar to those being built in West and Middle Germany. Thus the overall impression one gains when seeing these regions is that their landscape is still of German character.

As, according to the author's concept of geography, the character of the landscape is the most important criterion for the delimitation of regions and their grouping together into larger geographical units, he feels amply justified in including these areas in a geography of Germany, *Germany as a geographical region*, especially since at present there is no *de facto* German state as such and thus a geography of *Germany as a state* simply cannot be written.

Whether the *de facto* incorporation of these areas by Poland and the Soviet Union was justified and whether they will ever be part of a unified German state when it comes into being again (whenever that may be) are political though geographically relevant questions. Poland's claim to these areas on historic grounds—they were termed in Poland "regained territories"—are extremely weak. The United Kingdom would have more justification in claiming extensive parts of France, or Poland itself vast parts of Russia which were at later times part of a Polish state. If there is a justification it is that Poland more than any other country suffered terribly under German rule during the Second World War and that it deserved a compensation. That it was compensated in this way was in the last instance not Poland's choice but imposed on this unhappy state by Stalin. As for a return of these areas to a German state, one can only say that no responsible person could wish to uproot the people who have had to make it their home and where a large proportion of the population have since been born. The sooner Germans and Poles acknowledge these facts and try sincerely to overcome the tragic past the better for both of them. There are some hopeful signs that this is being realised.

This new block of flats at Leipzig clearly shows the influence of Russian architecture. Although this "Stalinesque" style is no longer used, it has left its distinctive mark in the townscapes of Middle Germany.

11. North Middle Germany

Since 1952 when for the purpose of centralising administration the nominally self-governing Länder, which in this case had been Mecklenburg, Brandenburg and the northern section of Saxony-Anhalt—mostly carved out of the former Prussian state—were abolished, this region has consisted politically of the districts of Rostock, Schwerin, Neubrandenburg, Potsdam, Frankfurt-on-Oder and a part of Magdeburg as well as West and East Berlin. (The latter is referred to in the G.D.R. as "Berlin, Capital of the German Democratic Republic.") Although West Berlin is according to the West German standpoint a Land of the Federal Republic—according to the G.D.R. authorities it is "A special political unit on the territory of the G.D.R."—and although the two parts of Berlin have since 1961 been divided by "the Wall" there are still certain aspects (e.g. freedom of movement of the forces of all the former Allies in the entire city) according to which Berlin as a whole forms a political unit with a special status.

Major cities (in thousands) arranged according to number of inhabitants in 1939:

	1939	1968
Berlin	4338·8	3233·6
West Berlin	2750·5	2149·7
East Berlin	1588·3	1083·9
Potsdam	135·9	110·7
Rostock	121·2	192·0
Brandenburg	83·7	92·3
Frankfurt-on-Oder	83·7	60·2
Schwerin	64·6	93·8
Stralsund	52·9	70·7

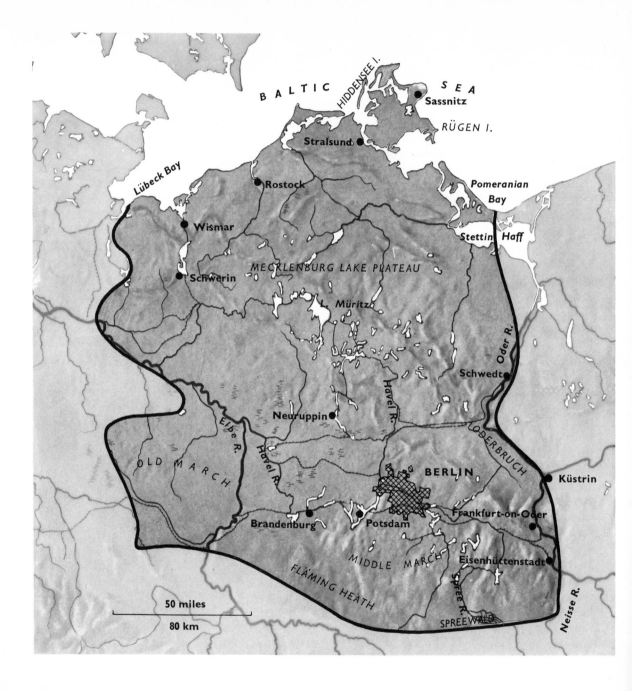

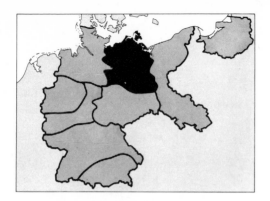

A coastline with natural harbours does not necessarily give rise to ports if the hinterland has no need of them. The coast of Middle Germany is a clear illustration of this simple truth. Between Lübeck and Stettin (Szczecin) the coast shows many indentations which resulted from the drowning of a hummocky ground moraine surface during the post-glacial rise of the level of the Baltic Sea. There are indeed a number of ports but even the largest of these, Rostock, had remained quite unimportant since the days of the Hanseatic League; its pre-war turnover was only about half a million tons. Since the immediate hinterland of this coast was exclusively agricultural there was little need for outlets, except for some grain, or for inlets for seaborne trade; the industrial regions farther inland looked to Lübeck and Stettin for their outlet to the Baltic, and to Hamburg and Bremen for their North Sea and world trade.

The division of Germany in 1945 has greatly affected these formerly sleepy ports. The "Iron Curtain" to the west and the Oder–Neisse line to the east, by cutting off Lübeck and Stettin, have provided the

The "New" Ports of Mecklenburg

Mecklenburg coast with a hinterland of unprecedented size and activity. As a result not only have all these harbours greatly increased their turnover, but being now the only ports of the G.D.R. they have developed commercial links with many more countries than before the war, and the composition of their imports and exports has also greatly changed. The export of potash salt fertiliser from the mines of Thuringia and Saxony, which before the war went largely through Bremen, Hamburg and Lübeck, is now concentrated at Wismar. It was the port with the greatest immediate expansion and the first to exceed a turnover of 2 million tons (in 1960). Since then it has declined somewhat (1968: 1·73 million tons). The reason for this was that a brand-new ocean port was constructed at the Warnow river estuary to the north of the old town of Rostock, and that this port has been attracting an increasing amount of trade. When it was first opened in 1960 its turnover was less than half a million tons, in 1968 the amount was 7·0 million tons. The total turnover of all the ports together—which in 1955 had been a mere 2·3 million tons—is anticipated to amount to about 13 million tons by 1970. Apart from potash salt exports most of the turnover (in weight) is bulk imports: mineral oil, iron ore, coal, grain, timber (in that order). A drawback for all the ports was inadequate communication links with the hinterland. At least the railway between Berlin and Rostock has been improved

greatly, but plans to build a canal from Rostock to the river Elbe and a motorway to Berlin have been shelved.

Another change for these ports is that they have now become the home ports of a sizeable merchant and fishing fleet, both of which had to be built up from scratch. The State Shipping Company was founded in 1952; in 1968 it had at its disposal 162 vessels with a total gross tonnage of 776,700. Before the war there had only been coastal fishing; now the trawlers of the G.D.R., whose home ports are for the most part Rostock and to a smaller extent the ferry port Sassnitz on the island of Rügen, sail to all important fishing grounds of the world. The catch rose from 37,000 tons in 1951 to 291,000 tons in 1968. All the trawlers and floating fish factories which go with them to the fishing grounds, and also a high proportion of the merchant ships are less than ten years old: in fact most ships were built in shipyards of these ports. Rostock has a long tradition in shipbuilding—its Neptun shipyard was the first in Germany to build propeller-driven iron ships. It still exists under this name today, but in addition there are new shipyards on the Warnow estuary, at Wismar, and for fishing vessels, at Stralsund. The construction of these passenger ships and freighters of 5,000 to 20,000 gross tons is one of the tasks allotted to the G.D.R. within Comecon (Council for Mutual Economic Aid)—the "Soviet Bloc Economic Community". Thus well over half the ships built here go to Comecon member countries.

As a subsidiary to shipbuilding the

making of diesel engines was started at Rostock, and over the last few years the city (and the G.D.R. tourist office) has made increasing efforts to attract foreign tourists to its "Baltic Week" held in mid-July. With all this new activity in the ports it is not surprising that they are amongst the few cities of the G.D.R. that have shown substantial growth. This growth found its visible expression in much new building, in particular the establishment of three dormitory satellite towns of Rostock.

While commerce and industry are reshaping the Mecklenburg coast, its immediate hinterland, boulder clay hills interspersed with many lakes, has remained completely agricultural. The northern part, with its heavy soils where the forests were cleared by the German settlers during the early stages of the eastern colonisation, is particularly fertile. Round villages, street villages and a variant of the forest villages are the traditional types of rural settlement, but with the growth of large estates, many developed into "estate villages" inhabited only by agricultural labourers, while the buildings of the estate and the *Herrenhaus* (manor house) in its park dominated the scene. Since the expropriation of the estates many of these houses have been used as quarries for building materials and the parks have been neglected.

Apart from Schwerin, with a population approaching 100,000, many of whom are engaged in engineering, food processing and chemical industries, the towns of Mecklenburg, at one time centres of the German colonisation, have remained small and are of importance only as local market centres.

The city of Stralsund was an important member of the Hanseatic League. After its decline Stralsund experienced a period of stagnation and there was therefore little new building. It was fortunate to get through the Second World War unscathed and has thus become the best example of an Hanseatic city. Its architectural importance has been recognised by designating the old part in its entirety as an ancient monument.

Stralsund is linked by a bridge and a causeway which carry road and rail to the island of Rügen, visible on the upper picture in the background. In this picture the Rostock-built rail and car ferry *Sassnitz* can be seen docking at Sassnitz, the Rügen terminal of the service to Trelleborg in Sweden. On the far right is part of the fishing port, the second most important of the G.D.R.

Heath and Sand of Brandenburg

South of the heights of the Baltic moraines with their beautiful lakes, we enter the more austere and monotonous landscape of Brandenburg. Instead of heavy, fertile boulder clay soils, much of the ground is covered with outwash material which has earned it the nickname of "God's sandbox". Dark pinewoods—the only way the poorest soils can be used—cover more than a third of the total area. In the centre is the region known as the Middle March. Across it run two of the *Urstromtäler* (see page 28), the valleys of an earlier period; prior to being drained, they were swampy and impassable areas. These valleys separated from each other a number of loam and sand plateaux, areas of easier cultivation and so of earlier settlement.

Reclamation of the swamps began in the early eighteenth century, when the marshes west of Berlin were drained, and reached a climax with the recovery of the Oderbruch (-*bruch* means swamp) which began some fifty years later. The Oderbruch is the section of the Oder Valley where the Oder follows an *Urstromtal* from Küstrin (Kostrzyn) to the point where it breaks through the Baltic Heights. Twelve hundred families in over forty new villages found a home where formerly water-birds had reigned, and Frederick the Great could say with justifiable pride that he had gained a whole province without fighting a war. These swamplands, when reclaimed, proved very fertile, and the Oderbruch became the granary of Brandenburg. Here wheat is grown, not merely rye as on the poorer soils, and also sugar-beet and tobacco.

The proximity of Berlin is clearly reflected in the land-use of Brandenburg. As one approaches Berlin there is an increase in fruit- and vegetable-growing both in the open and under glass, and the city's sewage water is used to make this very intensive cultivation possible.

The dominating role of Berlin in Brandenburg is seen in many other ways also. All railways, roads and canals lead to the capital, whose overriding importance hampered the growth of the other towns of this region. Potsdam is only an apparent exception since it owes much of its recent growth to Berlin, to which it is linked by

Of the new industrial locations the one most important in the long run is at Schwedt where a modern papermill—shown here—and an oil refinery (of which it was forbidden to take photographs) have been built. The latter uses oil imported from the Soviet Union by pipe-line. Operations commenced in 1964. In 1966 the through-put of the plant was doubled to 4 million tons per year. A pipe-line for refined products to the Leuna chemical works near Leipzig is nearly completed.

On the large State and collective farms, such as this one at Neuruppin in Brandenburg, milking on the pasture grounds obviates the twice-daily drive to the milking sheds.

a frequent suburban train service. Since August 1961, however, it has been cut off from West Berlin; and the train from East Berlin, referred to as "Sputnik" since it "orbits" West Berlin, takes about two hours instead of the previous half-hour. Once a garrison and the royal summer residence, it has recently also developed its own industrial life. It is the site of a railway engine construction plant, the largest in the G.D.R., and of a factory making all kinds of dental equipment. In addition the Babelsberg studios, to which is also attached a "Film College", make it the centre of the film industry of the G.D.R.

Of the other towns only Brandenburg to the west and Frankfurt-on-Oder to the east exceed 50,000 people. Brandenburg on the Havel river, until 1488 the residence of the territorial ruler of the margraviate (later electorate) of Brandenburg, has preserved many vestiges of its past, the most outstanding being the cathedral dating from the twelfth century and the fifteenth-century town hall. In

The two landmarks of the city of Brandenburg are its beautiful Gothic town hall with the Roland statue in front, and its modern steel plant.

One of the strangest landscapes of Brandenburg is the Spreewald to the south of Berlin, a swamp forest where until recently the principal means of transport was the punt as seen in this photograph. In this inaccessible area a few thousand Sorbs (or Wends) have preserved their Slav language and national customs. Though given every protection—even all the place-names on road signs are in Sorb and German—a continuing population influx as a result of industrialisation will inevitably lead to their assimilation.

recent history it has become an important manufacturing town and despite war damage and dismantling has retained this role after 1945. The steelworks and rolling-mills were rebuilt and the former Opel (General Motors) commercial vehicle plant, which was dismantled and shipped to Russia, was re-equipped to produce agricultural tractors. Other industries found at Brandenburg are heavy engineering and shipbuilding, and also light industries like leather and textiles. Frankfurt-on-Oder was traditionally a market centre, garrison town and administrative centre with little manufacturing industry. Located on the new Oder frontier and severed from its suburb to the east of the Oder it lost in population and importance. The fact that most of the trade between the G.D.R. and the Soviet Union (as far as it goes by rail) passes through Frankfurt's marshalling yards seems to have helped little. Of greater benefit was the establishment of an important component factory of the electronics industry, a semiconductor plant.

The main development on the Oder river took place to the south of Frankfurt at the terminus of the Oder–Spree Canal. Having lost the supplies of pig-iron and steel from the Ruhr (and Upper Silesia) it was decided, despite the lack of an adequate raw material base, to make the creation of an extensive iron- and steel-making capacity the king-pin of the first "Five Year Plan". The major project was the "EKO" (Eisenhüttenkombinat Ost) works, originally called "The Joseph Stalin Iron and Steel Combine" which together with a new town, Stalinstadt, to house the workers, the "first socialist town of Germany", was built from 1951 onwards

near the old town of Fürstenberg on Oder. As the iron ore has to be brought by train from the Soviet Union (and owing to the difference in gauge has to be reloaded at the Russo-Polish border), and most of the coal contrary to original plans does not come by water from Upper Silesia but is again brought by rail from Russia, this is a high-cost location. At last the steelworks originally planned for completion during the 1950s have started operating in 1967, avoiding at least another costly rail transport—taking the pig-iron to the Brandenburg steelworks—and the equally costly necessity of reheating. However, even after completion of the rolling-mills which is now anticipated for 1972 the EKO Works will remain a white elephant, impressive certainly, but doomed to operate at a loss if costs are realistically calculated. The socialist planners have at last realised this and a recent proposal envisages that pig iron production should cease in the near future. The new town whose name had become an embarrassment was combined with Fürstenberg, and both together given the new name of Eisenhüttenstadt (iron smelter town). However, this town which is approaching 40,000 inhabitants is now new in name only, since about half the built-up area dates at least from the period before the Second World War. There was thus not quite as much justification as was claimed for its twinning with a new town in Britain. At any rate this relationship with Crawley New Town has come to a sudden end as Crawley Council renounced it as a protest against the participation of G.D.R. troops at the Russian occupation of Czechoslovakia in August 1968.

Comparing the housing of the post-war part of Eisenhüttenstadt, i.e. the part that was originally the new town of Stalinstadt, with new towns in Great Britain, one is surprised that it consists almost exclusively of large blocks of flats even though the town lies on poor soils of little agricultural value. The blocks of flats shown here are characteristic of the Stalinesque style which prevailed until the mid 1950s. Later buildings in Eisenhüttenstadt are much more pleasing in design.

As destruction of the centre of Berlin—its "city"—was very extensive and because the boundary runs close to it rebuilding was extremely slow to start. Instead former sub-centres became the hubs of each respective part. In West Berlin it was around the Kürfürstendamm near the Zoo station, the terminus of trains from West Germany; in East Berlin it was the Alexanderplatz. Close by lies East Berlin's first major area of reconstruction, the Karl-Marx-Allee (or Stalin-Allee as it was originally called). The fortress like buildings which flank the entrance to it can be seen in the right background of this view. The avenue, with its atrocious "Stalinesque" architecture has become a source of embarrassment. Much more pleasing are the blocks of flats in the middle ground which date from the early 1960s; and with the buildings in the foreground, the "House of Teachers" and the circular shaped Congress Hall, the architecture of East Berlin has reached the stage where it is in no way inferior to that of the West. These buildings are part of a major scheme for reconstructing an extensive area, scheduled for completion in 1970. In its centre stands an impressive showpiece, a 361·5-metre television tower, the second highest structure in Europe.

Berlin

If anyone had ventured to prophesy that a city could be damaged beyond imagination, divided politically into two parts with one of these sealed off from the other and its hinterland, and still survive, nobody would have believed him. But this is exactly what has happened to Berlin.

Shortly after reaching its peak of importance Berlin began its decline. Many bombing raids and the battle for its possession until its conquest by the Red Army caused unparalleled destruction of housing and commercial and industrial premises and serious damage to many of its historic buildings. Most of these have been rebuilt, but in East Berlin the ruins of the Royal Palace were pulled down to make space for the Marx-Engels-Platz, a huge square for party rallies and parades.

The Berliners were allowed to elect their own government, unlike "Potsdam Germany" as a whole which came under an overall administration by the Allies. Alas, neither was to last when the "Cold War" began. The Russian representatives walked out of the "Kommandatura"; the acting Mayor of Berlin and the non-Communist councillors were barred from the town hall where, under Russian protection, a Communist city council was set up on 30 November 1948. But even before this happened and the division became an established fact, the Russians, on 24 June, began a blockade of West Berlin to force its integration into their occupation zone. The city was cut off from electricity, coal, food and all other essential supplies, but the combined determination of the West Berliners and the Western Powers ensured the success of the "airlift"—the almost incredible feat of supplying about 2 million people for over ten months, by air alone, with the basic requirements for their life and work.

The blockade failed, West Berlin retained its freedom; but the division of the city has become more and more pronounced. Not only are there two different currencies, separate public services and communication systems but, despite the closest possible personal ties, there is now very little movement through the seven checkpoints to which it has been restricted since August 1961. In the first years after the war there were still many people—in 1949 they numbered 150,000—who lived in one part of Berlin and worked in the other, now hardly any are allowed to do so. The main reason is that too many others—up to a thousand a day in the last months of the open boundary—went to West Berlin and did not return, preferring to become refugees. This constant loss of population, amounting *in toto* to nearly 3½ million, put an intolerable strain on the struggling economy of the G.D.R. Thus on 13 August 1961 the boundary between East and West Berlin was sealed by the "People's Police" and subsequently the ugly and inhuman Wall was built. There can be no argument as to its main purpose, viz. to put a stop to the population losses, but by forbidding West Berliners also to cross, except in dire emergencies and when a special pass agreement is in operation, it is also used as a lever, so far unsuccessfully, to separate West Berlin, which in the official G.D.R. jargon is called "a special political unit on the territory of the G.D.R."[sic], from the Federal Republic.

Of West Berlin's reconstruction of residential areas the most impressive is the new Hansa quarter built in connection with the International Building Exhibition 1957. The architects of the three buildings in this view are Gropius (U.S.A.), Vago (France) and Aalto (Finland).

In its growth Berlin has absorbed seven towns and fifty-nine villages. Parts of these still survive, like this village church dating from about A.D. 1200.

The traveller coming by train from the West will arrive at the Friedrichstrasse station shown here. Close by the station building there is an "Intershop" where visitors from the West are encouraged by prices lower than in the countries of origin to spend currency on Western chocolate, cigarettes, cigars, alcoholic liquor, perfume, nylon stockings and shirts —goods only available to the residents, if at all, at prices up to eight times as high.

The town hall of Berlin (built 1870), situated in the Soviet sector, is now merely the administrative centre for East Berlin. Its old nickname "The red town hall" has now acquired a political significance. The seat of the West Berlin senate is in the town hall of the borough of Schöneberg.

The airlift of the Western Powers into West Berlin in 1948–49 frustrated the first Russian attempt to gain control over the entire city. The air bridge monument which commemorates this achievement, which very few people would at the time have thought possible, has with typical Berlin humour been nicknamed "the hunger rake".

The war has changed even the relief of Berlin. In the distance is one of the hills built from the rubble of the ruins. An even larger one, used for skiing in the winter, lies in the Grunewald on the western outskirts. Much of the rubble was, however, used in the rebuilding, either by salvaging bricks or by turning them into "brick split" as aggregate for concreting, since bringing bricks from West Germany is prohibitively expensive. No such problems in the supply of building materials exist in East Berlin since brickworks and cement works are close at hand. Nevertheless it took until 1969 to rebuild this former palace (lower picture) located next to the Opera, and on its ground floor is now a café of which any city could be proud.

The Brandenburg Gate (built 1789) which stands on the western limit of the built-up area of the old city centre has since August 1961 ceased to be a gateway. Ugly as the Wall looks, it does not tell the tragic message of the city's division as forcefully as in those cases where the boundary runs along a street and the houses facing it had their doors and windows bricked up or were pulled down with only the front walls up to first-floor level left standing. The lower picture taken in the notorious Bernauer Strasse shows this operation in progress. The two "People's Police", sten gun at the ready, are making sure that none of the labourers might attempt a dash to freedom. (Altogether about 150 people were shot dead in escape attempts.)

Ironically the two halves of Berlin, which up till the building of the Wall had been developing apart quite rapidly—a glittering West Berlin being built up as a shop-window of the West and a drab and pompous East Berlin to which gayness and lightheartedness were as alien as to a Trappist monastery—have now become more alike again. Since East Berlin is open to visitors from the West (including West Germany) this half of the city has now assumed the role of a shop-window and its appearance has improved greatly. Further, the fact that each half of Berlin carries out its rebuilding, urban renewal and further development on the assumption that one day the city will be reunited also contributes, so that, despite the Wall, the two halves develop on roughly parallel lines. When will Berlin become reunited or at least when will the Wall go? This is closely tied up with developments in world politics.

The solution propagated by the G.D.R. regime, the establishment of West Berlin as an "independent territory", is obviously unacceptable as it would amount to West Berlin being swallowed up in no time. Reunification of the city as a corollary of a joining together of the Federal and the Democratic Republics under a freely elected government is too unrealistic at the moment to contemplate. This leaves only the hope that increased prosperity in the G.D.R. and a more liberal regime will reduce the lure of the West so much that the boundary could be reopened without fear of a renewed exodus. Berlin as a whole can still be regarded in some respects—chiefly theoretical—as a political unit of its own. Although in practice but a few vestiges of such unity remain, there exists the superstructure of an international authority which could be resurrected at any moment and could transform Berlin into a unified city with its own government and simultaneously create close ties with both the G.D.R. and Federal Germany.

One of the remarkable new buildings of West Berlin is its "Kongresshalle" (Congress Hall). Designed by the American architect, Stubbins, it is a present from the United States to the city of Berlin. The modern architecture in both parts of the city, their historical buildings and the cultural events on either side of the Wall amply justify the slogan used to attract visitors "Berlin ist eine Reise wert" (Berlin is well worth the journey).

The original University of Berlin, whose main entrance is shown here, was founded in the early nineteenth century and is named after Wilhelm von Humboldt—the brother of the great geographer Alexander. It is located at "Unter den Linden" in East Berlin. With the division of the city a new university, called the "Free University", was founded in 1948 in the western sector of the city. Although it had from the start a much greater student participation in the running of its affairs than other German universities, it was in the later 1960s nevertheless the scene of the worst clashes between extremist students and the authorities. Berlin is not only a city of learning but also a city of the arts and music. Most of its famous museums and art galleries as well as the forty theatres including the State Opera and State Playhouse were situated in what became the Soviet Sector. One of these theatres became the Brecht Ensemble—possibly the best, certainly the best known of Berlin's post-war theatres. Also new is Berlin's best-known satirical cabaret "Die Stachelschweine" (porcupines), as to be expected, located in West Berlin. If there is one thing in which the authorities and for that matter most Germans on either side of the Iron Curtain agree it is that theatres are an essential part of life and deserve a substantial public subsidy. Theatres were thus also given priority in rebuilding: the State Opera in East Berlin and the Schiller Theatre in West Berlin (in the picture below) were rebuilt when there were still extensive areas of ruins around.

Less than half of West Berlin, which covers nearly 900 km², is a built-up area; gardens and fields, lakes, woods and parks provide space for the recreation of over 2 million people. Here is the "Summer Garden" seen from the Funkturm—a kind of small-scale Eiffel Tower. Nevertheless many, if not most, of the places where Berliners used to go for a weekend excursion are now closed to them. For their holidays most people leave the claustrophobic atmosphere of the beleaguered city. If they go by road their journey begins here at the Funkturm where the AVUS road—the first autobahn built in Germany—which leads to the only check-point by which one may leave West Berlin for a transit journey through the G.D.R. branches off from the West Berlin urban motorway system. Until June 1968 West Germans (and West Berliners) needed only an identity card for a transit. Now they, like all foreigners except for the armed forces of the Western Allies, must have a visa issued at the check-point. The consequent delays and additional expense will result in an even greater use of air-lines than is the case already. The buildings which surround the Funkturm—in the lower picture on the left—date from the mid 1930s and are part of the exhibition grounds used for trade fairs and similar events.

12. South Middle Germany

From 1945 until 1952 this region consisted politically of the Länder Thuringia and Saxony, the major part of Saxony-Anhalt and a small part of Brandenburg. After their abolishment to centralise the administration more firmly the region consists of the districts of Cottbus, Halle, Erfurt, Gera, Suhl, Dresden, Leipzig, Chemnitz (in 1953 renamed Karl-Marx-Stadt) and part of Magdeburg. As regional terms the names of the former Länder continue to be used.

Major cities (in thousands) arranged according to number of inhabitants in 1939:

	1939	1968
Leipzig	707·4	589·1
Dresden	630·2	500·2
Chemnitz (Karl-Marx-Stadt)	337·7	296·7
Magdeburg	336·9	268·3
Halle	220·1	262·7
Erfurt	165·6	193·9
Dessau	119·1	97·0
Plauen	111·9	82·0
Görlitz	93·8	88·1
Zwickau	85·2	127·5
Gera	83·4	110·7
Jena	70·6	84·7
Weimar	65·9	64·0
Cottbus	55·5	79·5

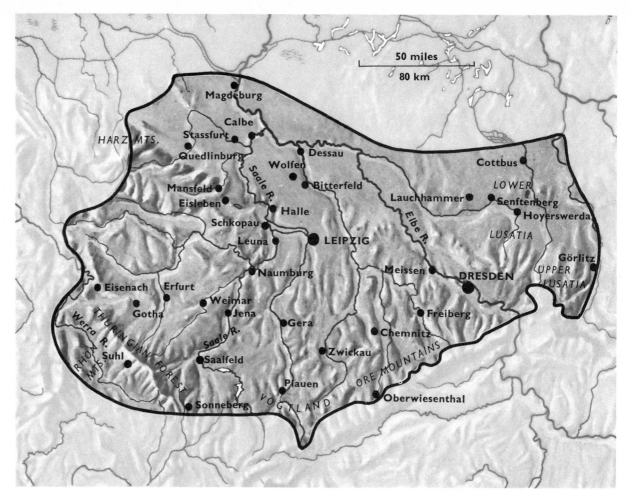

The southern part of Middle Germany illustrates the principle of unity in diversity. With a greatly varied physical background—it consists of the Saxon–Thuringian Bay and its mountain frame—and a diverse endowment of resources and scenery, it developed, mainly during the inter-war period, into a closely knit economic region which is now of decisive importance to the economy of the G.D.R.

Favoured by the excellent soils in the low-lying areas, which are based on loess, loam and marl, it is a region of ancient settlement where arable cultivation dates back to the Stone Age and intensive agriculture is of very great importance. There is no trace of woodland left on these fertile soils and huge fields of sugar-beet and wheat extend over Magdeburg *Börde*, the Golden Vale (south of the Harz) and the area around Leipzig, while the centre of Thuringia is also famous for its fruit and for flowers, cultivated in large fields mainly for their seeds.

Cities of Trade and Industry

In addition to its fertile soils this region has benefited by two major ancient west–east trade routes which pass through it, north and south of the Harz, intersecting two similar ones going north from Bohemia and Bavaria. The existence of these stimulated the early growth of towns, particularly of Leipzig, which owed to its trade its supremacy over the other cities; its twice-yearly fairs became the most important in Germany. In an excellent nodal location it developed into the largest city of this region. Leipzig was also the leading centre of printing and publishing in Germany, a position it has lost since 1945, whereas as a centre of industry—mechanical and electrical engineering, the manufacture of textiles and musical instruments—it has regained its former importance. The last of these industries is closely linked with its great musical tradition as the city of Johann Sebastian Bach, the birthplace of Richard Wagner, and the seat of a famous orchestra and academy of music.

Fairly close to Leipzig lies another major town of this region, Halle. It is an earlier foundation and on the basis of its salt wells (*Hal* means salt) it gained considerable wealth and was originally of greater importance than Leipzig. Physical factors do not,

Farming in the Magdeburg *Börde* is highly mechanised, especially in the larger of the "agricultural production associations", i.e. collective farms modelled on the Russian *kolkhozy*. In 1952 only 60 combine harvesters were in operation in the entire G.D.R.; by 1967 there were 17,000.

More than twenty-five years after the end of the war, ruins of churches in the city centre juxtaposed with extensive areas of new buildings and open spaces where houses once stood indicate how terribly Magdeburg suffered. Unfortunately much of the new building is in the "Stalinesque" style like the combined housing and commercial blocks shown here.

The size of Leipzig's railway station—the largest in Europe—is an indication of its former importance as a trade and communications centre. Now generally much quieter, it awakes to the old hustle and bustle during the famous fairs which, apart from their business function, have become an occasion for friends and relations from different sides of the "Iron Curtain" to meet.

Chemnitz, the "German Manchester" could hardly be called a beautiful city. Owing to its vigorous growth during the latter part of the nineteenth century, when the old fortifications were swept away, and wartime bombing, which left the city centre in ruins, hardly any medieval vestiges remain. Even the ground-plan of the city centre has changed greatly; the open space in front of the "new" (nineteenth-century) town hall, shown here, was created by clearing away the rubble of ruined buildings.

Medieval mining and trade gave rise to a number of cities in and around the **Harz Mountains**. By-passed by modern industry, they have preserved their old features as this street in **Quedlinburg**, another town which in its entirety has been designated an "ancient monument".

however, explain either why Halle, with its superior location on the Saale river, was overtaken by Leipzig, or why there are two major railway centres in such close proximity. The main reason for Leipzig's supremacy is that it was granted special privileges for its fairs in the Middle Ages; there are two railway centres because when the railways were built the two cities were situated in different territories, Saxony and Brandenburg-Prussia. Halle's growth is more recent, the result not only of its position as a major railway junction but also of recent development which has made it one of the foremost industrial centres of this region, dealing with sugar, salt, chemicals, iron and steel. Halle has nevertheless preserved many features of its pre-industrial era and with a university, a music academy (it is the birthplace of Handel), and an academy of sciences, it is a cultural centre as well.

Magdeburg situated on the northern fringe of this region, is as old as Halle. Though originally intended as a fortress (-*burg* means castle) it too profited greatly by the early trade. It became a centre for the advance of German settlers beyond the Elbe and its city charter served as a model for those of most of the towns and cities that came to be founded farther east, even far beyond the sphere where Germans settled speaking the German tongue. Today Magdeburg is not only the main market for the agricultural products, mainly sugar and grain, of the Magdeburg *Börde*, but, favoured by its location on the Elbe at the terminal point of the Mittelland Canal, it is an important commercial centre for many other commodities, especially potash, coal and timber. It is also of considerable industrial importance, the most notable of its industries being the making of heavy machinery.

Situated near the eastern margin of this region lies Dresden. Founded in the early thirteenth century, its first function was again that of a fortress, but as a bridge town it, too, shared in the early trade. The decisive factor in its development was that it became, towards the end of the fifteenth century, the residence of the rulers of Saxony. They made Dresden into a cultural centre with art collections, a notable opera-house and in appearance one of the most beautiful German cities. Its famous outstanding Baroque buildings were, alas, either destroyed or badly damaged in the most terrible air raids of the last war during the night of 13–14 February 1945 when about 135,000 people lost their lives.

Dresden and its environs also became the seat of important industries. The manufacture of its still famous porcelain was started in 1710 by one of its rulers; it was the earliest industry of its kind in Europe. The factory itself is in fact some way farther downstream at Meissen. Many of Dresden's industries are highly specialised, such as the manufacture of cigarettes and cigarette-making machines, the optical industry which pioneered the single-lens reflex camera and precision engineering. But with a small coalfield near by and its Elbe harbour for the handling of bulk commodities it has developed many other industrial activities as well.

Although Erfurt, the centre of Thuringia, is the oldest of the cities of South Middle Germany, in size it now holds only sixth place. It, too, was overshadowed by Leipzig and during the nineteenth century by the political situation, since as an island of Prussian territory it was divorced from its hinterland. Famous for the growing of flowers for seed and its international horticultural exhibition, it has also developed important industries, manufacturing office machinery, wirelesses, clothing and footwear.

Three more cities of this region now exceed 100,000 inhabitants: Gera, Chemnitz and Zwickau. Gera passed the 100,000 mark not so much as a result of genuine population growth, but through the incorporation in 1950 of thirty suburbs which were administratively independent until then. As a city it dates back to the thirteenth century; its modern industry has its roots in the influx of Dutch clothiers in the late sixteenth century. In the nineteenth century the manufacture of textile machines, and then general engineering, developed from its textile industry, and in terms of labour force the textile industry and engineering are now equal, but far ahead of all other industrial branches. Chemnitz (in 1953 re-named Karl-Marx-Stadt) resembles Gera in many respects but thanks mainly to its location on the Saxony coalfield, it became more important as a manufacturing town. The city takes its (old) name from the river on which it lies; it is not the successor to a Slav settlement but grew from a twelfth-century German monastic foundation. Its textile industry was originally based on local flax, but in the nineteenth century cotton became its principal raw material. Also in the nineteenth century mechanical engineering was developed, first to serve the needs of the textile industry, but then branching out into railway engine and vehicle building. Today engineering leads by far, the textile industry having been displaced to the city's hinterland. Zwickau, the oldest of the larger towns on the slope of the Ore Mountains is traditionally a mining town. Coal-mining in small quantities began in the fourteenth century, but originally more important was silver-mining on the nearby "Snowy Mountain". Equally important was its location on a trade route to Bohemia and the "high road" from Nuremberg to Dresden and Silesia. It is fortunate to have retained some architectural gems from these times like the former castle and the clothier's hall. Zwickau became important industrially with the increase of coal-mining during the nineteenth century, and during the inter-war period through its Auto Union motorworks. Although these have found their new home in Ingolstadt, West Germany, Zwickau again produces motor cars—the Trabant, the "Mini" of the East European countries.

In addition to these major towns there are many smaller ones, all medieval foundations with traditions of craftsmanship which were later an important factor in the general industrialisation of the whole region. Jena is famous for its optical industry (Zeiss) which employs 22,000 people; Gotha through its geographical and cartographical publishing firm founded in 1785; the mining town of Eisleben as the birthplace of Luther; Naumburg for its magnificent cathedral. Textile industries—the manufacture of woollens, carpets, embroidered goods or lace—give importance to the towns of Plauen, Görlitz and Cottbus.

Meissen, one of the oldest cities of Saxony, is dominated by its Gothic cathedral and the Albrecht castle. After Böttger had discovered in 1707 the secret of making bone china—formerly only procurable from the Far East—the castle was used from 1710 to 1860 for the manufacture of the famous "Dresden" china.

Mineral Wealth

There was another reason apart from communications which attracted many people to South Middle Germany in the Middle Ages; this was the wealth of metals in its mountain frame. Silver and copper as well as lead, zinc and iron, have been mined in the Harz since the tenth century and this mining activity led to a great deal of woodland clearing (there are many place-names incorporating *roden* which means "to clear") and the establishment of mining villages and towns at considerable altitudes. The same is true of the Ore Mountains (Erzgebirge) where mining began around the year 1200. This area became an early training-ground for those practising mining and metallurgy; miners from the Harz and the Ore Mountains were mining pioneers from the thirteenth century onwards not only in Bohemia, Tirol, Transylvania and the Rhineland, but also overseas. The earliest mining college in the world is at Freiberg in the Ore Mountains. On the Bohemian side of the Ore Mountains, also until 1945 an area of German settlement, Joachimsthal was an important silver-mining town and the silver coins minted there in the sixteenth century became known as *Thaler*, which in the English language became "dollar".

When huge quantities of silver were imported from the New World and as the ore bodies became worked out, mining dwindled away after the Thirty Years War and has survived only in a few places. The most important of them today is the Mansfeld district

A view from the Fichtelberg in the Ore Mountains to Oberwiesenthal which, at an altitude of some 1,000 metres is the highest German town. The Ore Mountains are the most densely settled of the German Uplands and consequently most of their original mantle of forest was cleared long ago. Mining, which originally brought settlement up to these heights, has been resumed—the centre of uranium mining being at Aue, about 32 kilometres north-west of Oberwiesenthal.

Mining sometimes gives rise to strange landscapes. At first glance this pictu[re] seems to show an Egyptian pyramid, but it is in fact a spoilheap of a copper o[r] mine in the eastern Harz Foreland, typical Börde country. While the huge fiel[d] indicate that most of the land belongs to a collective farm, a few strip fields in th[e] left middle ground show that in 1959, when this picture was taken, some farme[r] had still resisted the pressure to join the collective.

Brown coal is by far the main source of energy and still a very important raw material for the chemical industry in the G.D.R. As early as 1946 production exceeded that of pre-war years, and in 1964 257 million tons were produced—the maximum reached so far. Since then, contrary to plans, there was a decline (to 242 million tons) and the target of 300 million tons by 1970 has been abandoned. Mining is highly mechanised and uses giant excavators like those shown here, and only open-pit mines have continued in production.

The original attractions for settling the Thuringian Forest were its resources of iron and copper. Mining has now virtually ceased, but it left as an inheritance a widespread, highly specialised, manufacturing industry. An example of this is found in the small town of Lauscha (above) which developed from a sixteenth-century glassworks. It now specialises in the manufacture of glass Christmas tree decorations, thermometers and (human) glass eyes.

in the eastern foothills of the Harz, which at one time supplied the copper for most of Europe. Copper-mining has lately been greatly increased and the G.D.R. is able to produce sufficient to satisfy its own requirements. Mining on a large scale returned to the Ore Mountains after 1945. A labour force estimated at 50,000 is engaged there and near Gera in the mining of uranium ore, the chief source of atomic energy.

Geographically, the decline in mining was important because many people who had formerly depended on it had to find another means of livelihood; agriculture alone was insufficient to support them all. In the process of adjustment a great number of cottage industries arose in which the raw materials account for only a fraction of the cost of the finished articles; highly skilled work is the important factor. Examples of this are lace-making, which became widely practised in the Ore Mountains, toy-making, for which the Sonneberg district in the Thuringian Forest is famous, or, in the Vogtland, the making of musical instruments, a craft which developed from the making of violins.

These various strands—intensive agriculture, trade, a tradition

in mining and metallurgy, relative over-population and development of cottage industry—all still separate in the middle of the last century, combined to make South Middle Germany, under the impact of the Industrial Revolution, the most varied, intensively industrialised, major region of Germany and, in its centre, the most densely settled. Two resources, previously of no value, were responsible for this development: brown coal and potash salt.

Brown coal was the first to become important. It occurs in layers about 16 metres thick, increasing at times to as much as 115 metres, and at depths of from 12 to 65 metres throughout almost the entire Leipzig Bay. A second, independent, major field is situated in Lusatia, west of the Neisse, with Senftenberg as its centre. Its earliest use was as fuel in the saltworks of Halle in the late eighteenth century. The mining was mostly open pit, and its chief exploitation came with the development of the beet-sugar industry and the consequent demands for fuel. The invention of briquette-making, which made brown coal more economic to transport, was a second stimulus; in fact the rapidly growing city of Berlin was largely heated by brown coal from this region. Later, with the

The coking plant at Lauchhammer in Lusatia, built in 1952–7, produces about 1 million tons of brown coal high-temperature (B.H.T.) metallurgical coke per year. Although this saves coke (and pig-iron) imports, the production of B.H.T. coke is a long and costly process. Since, furthermore, it has to be used in fairly small blast-furnaces, the pig-iron at the Calbe ironworks where these have been built must have been about the most expensively produced in the world.

swift rise of electricity to importance, giant power stations were built, consuming large amounts of brown coal and supplying Berlin and the entire region with electric current. Then came the development of the chemical industry using brown coal directly as a raw material and indirectly as a source of energy. The most recent use for brown coal was a source of coke. It was realised, however, that production costs when smelting with it were prohibitive and the "low shaft" blast furnaces at Calbe have shut down.

Both fields together produce now about 250 million tons of brown coal a year. It is likely that the quantity mined will remain of that order of magnitude, but gradually the emphasis of production which lay in the Leipzig Bay is shifting to Lusatia. However, in both areas the resulting mining landscape is similar: huge open pits, towering chimneys of the briquetting plants and electric power stations, their cooling towers and—dating from the period when brown coal was used as a source of petrol products—the hydrogenation plants with their maze of pipes and their storage globes and tanks.

The vast salt deposits, sediments of the Permian Sea—which are also to be found almost everywhere in the Lowland Bay—provided the last great stimulus to industrialisation. It is true that common salt had been produced for centuries; but common salt was only of minor importance to industrial development. It was the potash salt, previously thrown away, which gained industrial significance with the development of chemistry. In addition, potash salts came to be of great importance as artificial fertiliser for the improved agriculture which went hand-in-hand with industrial expansion. Germany is still the leading producer of these minerals, although it no longer has the monopoly that it had before 1914. Production is divided almost equally between Middle Germany, where extraction originally began after 1850, and Western Germany, where it spread subsequently. Each area produces about 20 million tons of raw salt annually.

Intensive and varied agriculture with food industries in the Lowland, subsistence agriculture with cottage industries in the Uplands, the large-scale textile industry in a continuous belt from the upper Saale to the Neisse, the mining of copper ore, brown coal, salt and potash, briquetting, the generation of electricity, the chemical industry which includes the manufacture of synthetic rubber, fertilisers, dyes and plastics, drugs, synthetic fibres and photographic materials; even this list does not exhaust the many aspects of the region's economic life.

The region also possesses highly developed and widely distributed iron and steel industries, heavy industry as well as machine building and engineering. There are two main reasons for the development of these: first, the Zwickau coalfield, and, second, the demands for machinery and equipment by all the other industrial concerns. Also located in this region at Eisenach, Chemnitz and Zwickau is most of the G.D.R.'s motor industry. Before 1939 nearly a third of all the motor vehicles produced in Germany came from the area of the later Soviet Zone. Owing to dismantling, shortages of raw materials and factories producing components as well as a slower rise in living standards and an anti-car policy, the motor industry has recovered very slowly and its share of the total German production is now only about 3 per cent. (In 1965 when West Germany produced about 3 million motor cars the total number produced in the G.D.R. had just passed the 100,000 mark.) To buy a car in "socialist" Germany means a long wait and paying a price about five times as high as the export price of the same model to a "capitalist" hard-currency country. Even so, the G.D.R. is now by far the most highly motorised country of the Soviet bloc.

The Saxony coalfield is very small compared with the major coalfields of Germany, its annual production being only about 2 million tons, but as the only source of hard coal in the G.D.R. it is nevertheless of some economic importance. The shortage of coal which necessitates the import of about 9 million tons every year as well as about 3 million tons of coke (from Russia, Poland and Czechoslovakia) is a serious handicap, but the change-over to town gas produced from brown coal and supplied via a national gas grid (under construction) will alleviate it somewhat.

Another mineral resource, now in short supply but historically important, is iron ore. As its occurrences were either too small or of low iron content they did not give rise to a large-scale iron-making industry during the nineteenth century. In 1936 the share of pig-iron making of the later Soviet Zone area amounted only to 1·7 per cent of the total produced in Germany as a whole and was

The brown coal combine "Schwarze Pumpe" ("The black pump" is the name of a roadside inn near by) according to its works area of 25 square kilometres, is one of the mammoth industrial establishments of the G.D.R. This picture can only show a small section of this giant works which consist of electric power stations, briquetting plants and installations for gasification. Yet, despite having started production (of electricity) in 1959, this largest single project of the second "Five Year Plan" (1956–60) which is now history, Schwarze Pumpe is far from completed. Completion was originally scheduled for 1963; now it is 1972 at the earliest. Although its *raison d'être* had been the production of 2·5 million tons of metallurgical coke, none has been produced so far. It is still stated that it is to produce coke (the figure is now 1·8 million tons), but it is more than doubtful whether the coke ovens will ever be built. By producing large amounts of electricity, briquettes and town gas—it is to produce more than the entire 1961 gas production of the G.D.R.—it will play an important role for some time. However, with construction costs having almost doubled from the original estimate and, owing to the delays, being in parts obsolete even before completion, it can hardly be expected that it will pay its way: an awe-inspiring but uneconomic industrial dinosaur; a monument to the misconceived second "Five Year Plan". Since the air pollution from burning these millions of tons of brown coal is very bad, the workers—there are to be 16,000 altogether—are housed about 25 kilometres away at Hoyerswerda, "the second socialist town of Germany". This town, which in 1939 had just over 7,000 inhabitants, was by 1967 approaching the 50,000 mark and has thus more claim to being a "new town" than Eisenhüttenstadt.

The Rappbode Dam in the Harz, completed in 1960, which rises 88 m above the valley floor, has the distinction of being the highest in Germany. Its reservoir supplies water for domestic and industrial use to areas east of the Harz.

Next to the Soviet Union the G.D.R. is the most important producer of chemicals, plastics and synthetic fibres within Comecon. The district of Halle is the chemical district as it contains the Leuna works, the Buna (synthetic rubber) works at Schkopau, the photographic works at Wolfen (formerly Agfa, now called ORWO = original Wolfen), the mineral oil processing plant Lützkendorf, and the electro-chemical combine, Bitterfeld, of which a workshop is shown here. These works together employ about 90,000; a new town, the Halle-Neustadt, planned to have 70,000 inhabitants by 1973, is under construction to provide housing in close proximity to the Leuna and Buna works to minimise the present time loss in commuting from villages. (This new town, at its first appearance in the statistics in 1967, had 12,645 inhabitants.)

almost entirely due to the output of a single plant, the Maxhütte near Saalfeld in Thuringia. In the mistaken belief that it was necessary to develop a substantial iron- and steel-making capacity regardless of cost, the two new iron-smelting works already mentioned were built: the EKO at Eisenhüttenstadt and, in this region close to home-produced ores, the Eisenhüttenwerk West at Calbe. To supply this and the Maxhütte, iron ore mining was stepped up from about 400,000 tons to 1·7 million tons which satisfied about half the requirements of the iron smelters. This shortage and the shortage in the supply of iron and steel, where home production again satisfies only about 50 per cent of requirements is overcome by imports from the Soviet Union.

Although modern industry is the common and all-pervasive characteristic of this region, it has not succeeded in obliterating the many types of landscape arising from marked physical differences and earlier occupance. Thuringia and the Harz are probably the most attractive parts of South Middle Germany. Highly industrialised though the area is, the industry which has developed from craftsmen's workshops is mostly either cottage or small-scale. Consequently the countryside lacks the ugliness which is the inevitable concomitant of heavy industry and large factories of the older kind; in particular there is no open-cast mining of brown coal. The potash salt-mines and the wells of natural gas, which occurs in some quantity and is piped to industrial towns, do not make any comparable scars. There is still much woodland in the mountains and hills and this, as well as the great number of medieval castles and beautiful historic buildings in the towns, attracts many visitors.

Equally attractive, though for different reasons, is the Elbe Valley between Meissen and the Czechoslovakian border. The southern section of it is "Saxon Switzerland", so-called for its picturesque and mountainous character. The sandstones of which the valley sides and "turrets" (steine) are formed are widely quarried and attract the tourist and rock-climber.

In the northern section the Elbe Valley widens; it is a rift valley resembling that of the Rhine, though very much smaller. A fertile soil and sheltered position give rise not only to intensive arable cultivation but also to the growing of fruit, early vegetables and flowers, and on the sunny slopes there are even vineyards.

On leaving Bohemia the Elbe breaks through the Uplands in a deep gorge. Although formerly avoided by communication lines it is now followed by the main railway—though not the road—from Berlin to Prague and, since the clearing of rocks and obstacles, the Elbe has itself become an important waterway, one of the main freights being Czechoslovakian coal. In the summer months paddle steamers like the one shown here provide river trips for the great number of visitors.

13. The East

Politically until the beginning of the Second World War this region, apart from the territory of the Free City of Danzig, belonged within the German Reich to the Prussian State and consisted of its following provinces or parts: East Prussia, most of Pomerania, most of Silesia, eastern Brandenburg. Following the conquest of the area by the Red Army in 1944–5 and the agreements of Tehran and Yalta, they were, in March 1945, handed over to the government of Poland, except for East Prussia north of a west–east line from the middle of the Frische Nehrung, which was retained by the Soviet Union. Contrary to the Potsdam agreement of 1945, which stipulated that territorial transfers should await confirmation by a peace treaty, they have been fully incorporated into Poland and the Soviet Union respectively. Northern East Prussia became in July 1946—simultaneously with the renaming of Königsberg—Kaliningrad Oblast of the Russian S.S.R., while the other areas now make up ten of Poland's voivodeships either entirely or in parts.

Major cities (in thousands) arranged according to number of inhabitants in 1939:

	1939	1968
Breslau (Wroclaw)	629·6	509·4
Stettin (Szczecin)	383·0	331·7
Königsberg (Kaliningrad)	372·2	c. 262·0
Danzig (Gdańsk)	c. 250·0	364·0
Hindenburg (Zabrze)	126·2	199·3
Gleiwitz (Gliwice)	117·3	166·6
Beuthen (Bytom)	101·1	186·7
Elbing (Elblag)	86·0	86·0
Liegnitz (Legnica)	83·7	74·6
Waldenburg (Walbrzych)	64·1	126·2
Oppeln (Opole)	53·0	84·9
Allenstein (Olsztyn)	50·4	89·7
Landsberg on Warthe (Gorzów Wielkopolski)	48·1	70·3
Grünberg (Zielona Gora)	26·1	69·3

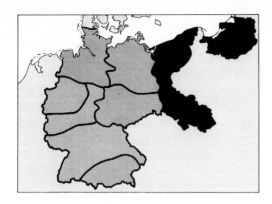

The most striking feature common to the human geography of this region is that since 1945 it has become mainly, though not entirely, inhabited by Slav peoples: Russians in the north-east, Poles and a few hundred thousand Ukrainians elsewhere. Despite the official Polish statistics to the contrary, there are still about 800,000 Germans there also. These inhabitants of 1945 were for various reasons classified by the Polish authorities as "autochthons", descendants of the indigenous Slav population of the past, and allowed or even forced to remain. Their assimilation is far from accomplished, and in many cases even children, born well after 1945, are brought up with German as their mother tongue. However, this proportion of possibly 10 per cent German population is not the reason for including these parts of the former German Reich in this account. The reason, as previously stated, is that on the whole the landscape (and townscapes) which was shaped by Germans has changed surprisingly little—at least in those parts which were incorporated into Poland—in many cases even less than between the Elbe and Saale, and is thus still a German cultural landscape. How long it will retain this character one cannot say; at the moment it looks as if it will be for a long time. To avoid any misunderstanding, it should also be stated that the inclusion of these areas in a geography of Germany neither means that they should not with equal justification be included in geographical accounts of Poland and the Soviet Union, nor that the character of the landscape (and equally the fact of having at some time in the past been part of a particular state) here or elsewhere in the world can justifiably be used as a basis for territorial claims.

The landscape changes that have taken place have on the whole been for the worse. With the emphasis on industry the industrial towns have sprouted rather unattractive new housing estates, while those parts of the towns which survived serious war damage, as well as small towns, villages and the countryside in general show definite signs of neglect: ruined buildings, a poor state of decoration and sizeable areas of uncultivated land.

From the Oder to the Memel

In the past Germans in the west and south often used to speak of Pomerania to indicate any far-away region, and except for its capital Stettin, which lies on its western margin, Pomerania was very little known. Not that its landscape lacks attractive features; one section of the morainic hills with its string of lakes was even known as the "Pomeranian Switzerland". On the whole, however, the countryside is unexciting, dominated by a mixture of coastal dunes, farmland on the boulder clay, beechwoods on the terminal moraines, and heathland and pinewoods on the sandy stretches south of them. The straight coastline did not favour the development of ports; along the whole stretch between Stettin and Gdynia there is now only one small commercial port, Kolberg. The generally meagre soil and the lack of mineral resources in the hinterland explain the absence of larger towns; only two of the few towns that do exist just exceed 50,000 inhabitants; and the main railway line from Berlin to Danzig skirts Pomerania in the south. All these factors contributed to make it a relative economic backwater.

Pomerania used to be a region where farms of over 100 hectares and estates of more than 200 hectares covered nearly a third of the agricultural land. Although the main reasons for this development were historical and social, it had been favoured by the nature of the land; the prevailing soils of medium to poor quality are best managed in larger farming units. Polish rule has brought a certain change in this respect. Except for over 700 large State farms, occupying one-third of the total agricultural land, the farmland was at first divided into small- and medium-sized holdings averaging 10 hectares. Many of these farms were, however, shortly afterwards combined again into large units, "agricultural production associations".

Under the "New Course" in 1956 these were broken up, but there is no knowing whether one day they may not be re-established.

Stettin (Szczecin), which before the war took third place amongst the German ports, owes its status as one of the leading Baltic ports to a number of factors. Situated at the mouth of the Oder it became, after the river was made navigable, the natural port for the industrial region of Upper Silesia, but it also acquired an important share of Berlin's overseas trade (being linked to the city by a large canal), as well as that of the South Middle German industrial region, and it even extended its hinterland into Czechoslovakia. The majority of the commodities handled—the total turnover before 1939 was about 8·5 million tons—were bulk cargo: grain, Swedish ore and Upper Silesian as well as Ruhr coal. The presence of ore and coal led to the establishment of heavy industry with blast-furnaces and rolling-mills which produced the steel for the graving yards, used for carrying out repairs to the largest vessels calling at the port. The little outport of Swinemünde (Swinoujscie) served as a passenger port, seaside resort, and naval base.

When the war ended extensive areas of Stettin lay in ruins. An air raid had destroyed the city centre in 1943 and the battle for the possession of Stettin in 1945 had caused further heavy damage. Considerable progress has been made in the rehabilitation of industrial installations and port facilities and the turnover of the port with nearly 14 million tons (1968) was more than half as much again as it was before the war. Gradually the city itself is also being rebuilt, but it will take some years more before one may be able to say that this has been accomplished. Swinemünde was fortunate to escape war damage. It is again a resort with its hotels and boarding-houses—many now owned by Polish trade unions—filled with guests in the summer. Since, however, it remained a naval base, now for units of the Soviet Navy, an entire residential quarter of "superior houses" was in 1967 still used for housing the Russian Navy officers and their families. It looked as if no maintenance had been carried out on these villas since they were taken over as military quarters: their gardens were overgrown, fences falling down, many window-panes broken, white arrows on the walls still pointing to the escape hatches of the air-raid shelters and even

Small market towns like Pyritz, south of Stettin, are indistinguishable from similar towns to the west of the Oder, whereas compared with street scenes of small towns in central or eastern Poland this view shows quite a different world. The differences are also apparent in the rural scene illustrated by a view from the Pomeranian Heights. There are signs, like untilled fields, that farming is now not as efficient as it could be, but the lay-out of the large fields is quite different from that of the smaller and more irregular traditional Polish ones beyond the formerly German-speaking lands.

situated largely on the left bank of the Oder. On these soils, agriculture came to be amongst the most intensive in Germany and a large surplus of wheat and sugar, as well as other agricultural products, left Silesia for the more western parts of Germany. It was in this Silesian *Börde* that the first beet-sugar refinery in the world was set up in 1880, an event which contributed to the revolution of European agriculture. These best soils had been cleared of forest and were being farmed before the arrival of the German pioneer-settlers in the late twelfth century, but the transformation of the less good soils from primeval forest to fields and meadows began with the coming of the Germans. Woodlands persisted only on the poorest soils, and were turned into well-tended forests which became the basis of a flourishing timber industry.

The taming of the Oder river, which forms the backbone of Silesia, is another German achievement. Heavy rains or rapid melting of snow in the Sudeten Mountains used to result in destructive floods, but now a number of barrages retain the flood water of tributaries in reservoirs. The Oder itself was confined between dykes, its course straightened, and its upper section made into a canal, so that it could serve as the waterway linking the Upper Silesian industrial region with the Baltic Sea as well as with the German canal system.

The undisputed regional hub of Silesia is Breslau (Wroclaw). Founded as a German city after the destruction of the former Slav town by the Mongols in 1241, it rose to importance as a centre of trade and later of industry. With a university and book-publishing houses it also acquired a cultural fame. Badly damaged during the war, it is still considerably smaller than it used to be, although much rebuilding has been done.

While Breslau owes its size to a number of factors, the only other towns of over 100,000 inhabitants are those whose essential economic bases are coal-mining and heavy industry. Apart from Waldenburg they all lie in Upper Silesia, which after 1945 became the power house for the transformation of Poland from an agricultural into an industrial state. With a production of about 120 million tons of coal in the late 1960s Upper Silesia has in this respect now overtaken the Ruhr and there are no signs of a coal crisis here. (This figure represents the production of the entire

The most outstanding building of Breslau—and one of the best German Gothic buildings apart from churches—is its town hall. It escaped serious damage during the Breslau siege and, like a number of old merchants' houses around the square at whose centre it stands, it has been carefully restored.

Although mining goes back to the sixteenth century, Waldenburg was originally known as a linen town. From about 1850 onwards, however, coal-mining became increasingly important. Nearby are also mining villages.

125

Some of the industrial towns of Upper Silesia have medieval beginnings and have preserved its pre-industrial core. One of these is Gleiwitz (Gliwice) which was founded in 1276 but is also important for the industrialisation of Upper Silesia from the very start. It was here that the first blast-furnace on the European continent began the smelting of iron ore in 1796. The picture taken from the steeple of its remarkable thirteenth-century church shows the feature characteristic of all old Silesian towns: a central market square, the Ring (in Polish now called Rynek) with the town hall occupying its centre. The buildings beyond show that the main growth of Gleiwitz took place much more recently and has continued into the present.

Upper Silesian coalfield of which the part retained by the German Reich after the First World War produced in 1938 about 30 million tons, compared with 38 million tons produced in the much larger part ceded to Poland.)

In January 1945 Upper Silesia fell virtually without battle to the rapidly advancing Red Army; thus little destruction occurred and coal-mining and industrial production hardly came to a halt. A very high proportion of the native population of Upper Silesia were accorded the status of "autochthons" and in the country they still form the majority of the inhabitants. Although this is not the case in the large industrial towns which have since grown substantially by migration from all over Poland, there is no difficulty even here in making oneself understood in German. The growth of the towns has been so rapid that construction of housing could not keep pace and the urgent task of replacing obsolete accommodation dating from the late nineteenth century, and classifiable only as slums, has not yet been tackled. For these reasons—absence of large-scale destruction or replacement of housing and the high degree of continuity between pre-1945 and the present—the landscape has virtually stayed as it was before this area became incorporated into Poland. The gravestones in the village cemeteries on well-tended graves still proclaim in German "Rest in Peace". It is peace more than anything else which this border zone from the Baltic Sea to the Sudeten Mountains most needs to heal its thousand wounds. May it be granted that peace.

A drawback of the Upper Silesian industrial area as compared with the Ruhr was the absence of a modern waterway linking its heart to the Oder like the Herne Canal links the Ruhr centre to the Rhine. Thus for shipment from and to Stettin and to Berlin, the river port of Cosel (shown here) developed at the virtual head of the Oder navigation. Though it is still used today—the picture was taken in 1967 —Koźle, as it is now called, has shrunk in importance since the completion of the Gleiwitz Canal in 1939 which enables barges up to 1,000 tons capacity to reach the coalfield itself.

Suggestions for further reading

In keeping with the introductory character of this book, most of the publications listed are in English. German atlases are, however, included since they can be used without a knowledge of German.

General References

M. Blacksell, "Recent changes in the morphology of West German townscapes" in E. W. Gilbert, *Urbanisation and its problems, essays in honour of E. W. Gilbert*, Oxford, 1968.

A. Bullock, *Hitler: a study in tyranny*, London, 1964.

J. H. Clapham, *The economic development of France and Germany*, Cambridge, 1963.

H. C. Darby, "The clearing of the woodlands in Europe", in W. L. Thomas (ed.), *Man's role in changing the face of the earth*, Chicago, 1956, 183–216.

R. E. Dickinson, *The German Lebensraum*, Harmondsworth, 1943.

——, "The development and distribution of the medieval German town", *Geography*, 27, 1942, 9–21, 47–53.

——, "The morphology of the medieval German town", *Geographical Review*, 35, 1945, 74–91.

——, "Rural settlements in the German lands", *Annals of the Association of American Geographers*, 39, 1949, 238–63.

——, "The political geography of Germany and Austria", in H. W. Weigert (ed.), *New compass of the world*, London, 1949, 172–91.

——, "The geography of commuting in West Germany", *Annals of the Association of American Geographers*, 49, 1959, 443–56.

——, *Germany: a general and regional geography*, London, 1961.

——, *The West European city*, London, 1961.

——, "Town-country relations in Germany", "Capitals and their regions in Germany", in *City and Region*, London, 1964, 88–98, 370–87, 529–53.

J. Dollfus, *Atlas of Western Europe*, London, 1962.

T. H. Elkins, "The brown coal industry of Germany", *Geography*, 38, 1953, 18–29.

——, "Oil in Germany", *Geography*, 45, 1960, 108–10.

——, *Germany*, London, 1968.

E. Fisher, "The passing of Mitteleuropa", in W. G. East, A. E. Moodie (ed.), *The changing world*, London, 1956, 60–79.

G. Frumkin, *Population changes in Europe since 1939*, London, 1952.

E. W. Gilbert, "The university town in England and West Germany", *The University of Chicago, Department of Geography, Research Paper*, 71, Chicago, 1961.

——, *Urbanisation and its problems, essays in honour of E. W. Gilbert*, Oxford, 1968.

T. Greene, "West German city reconstruction", *Sociological Review*, 7, 1959, 231–44.

G. Hallett, "Agricultural policy in West Germany", *Journal of Agricultural Economics*, 19, 1968, 87–95.

C. C. Held, "Refugee industries in West Germany", *Economic Geography*, 32, 1956, 316–35.

J. Hennessy (and others), *Economic "miracles". Studies in the resurgence of the French, German and Italian economies since the second world war*, London, 1964.

A. M. Lambert, "Farm consolidation in Western Europe", *Geography*, 48, 1963, 31–48.

R. E. H. Mellor, "The integration of the German refugees", *Advancement of Science*, 11, 1955, 465–74.

——, "The German refugee problem: ten years retrospect", *Scottish Geographical Magazine*, 73, 1957, 1–18.

H. C. Meyer, *Mitteleuropa in German thought and action*, The Hague, 1955.

E. Otremba (ed.), *Atlas der deutschen Agrarlandschaft*, Wiesbaden, 1962.

W. N. Parker, "Entrepreneurship, industrial organisation and economic growth: a German example", *Journal of Economic History*, 14, 1954, 380–400.

E. J. Passant, *A short history of Germany, 1815–1945*, Cambridge, 1959.

N. Perry, "Recent developments in the West German oil industry", *Geography*, 52, 1967, 408–11.

G. Pfeifer, "The quality of peasant living in Central Europe", in W. L. Thomas (ed.), *Man's role in changing the face of the earth*, Chicago, 1956, 240–77.

N. J. G. Pounds, "Divided Germany and Berlin", *Van Nostrand Searchlight Books*, Princeton, 1962.

Press and Information Office of the Federal Government, *Germany reports*, Wiesbaden, annually.

——, *The economic pattern of modern Germany*, London, 1963.

M. J. Proudfoot, *European refugees 1939–52*, London, 1952.

F. Redlich, "Recent developments in German economic history", *Journal of Economic History*, 18, 1958, 516–30.

D. S. Rugg, "Post-war progress in cartography in the Federal Republic of Germany", *Cartographic Journal*, 2, 1965, 75–84.

R. G. Schmidt, "Post-war developments in West German agriculture 1945–53", *Agricultural History*, 29, 1955, 147–59.

P. Schöller, "The division of Germany—based on historical geography?", *Erdkunde*, 16, 1965, 161–4.

K. A. Sinnhuber, "Central Europe, Mitteleuropa, Europe Centrale: an analysis of a geographical term", *Institute of British Geographers, Transactions and Papers*, 20, 1954, 15–39.

——, "The representation of disputed political boundaries in general atlases", *Cartographic Journal*, 1, No. 2, 1964, 20–8.

Statistisches Bundesamt (ed.), *Die Bundesrepublik Deutschland in Karten*, Mainz, 1965.

G. Stolper (and others), *The German economy: 1870 to the present*, New York, 1967.

A. J. P. Taylor, "The course of German history", *University Paperbacks*, London, 1961.

M. Tracy, *Agriculture in Western Europe*, London, 1964.

C. Troll, "'Sölle' and 'Mardelles'. Glacial and periglacial phenomena in continental Europe", *Erdkunde*, 16, 1962, 31–4.

United Nations, "Structural adaptation in Eastern and Western Germany", *Economic Bulletin for Europe*, 8, 1956, 45–89.

S. Van Valkenburg, "The rise and decline of German 'Lebensraum'", in H. W. Weigert (ed.), *New compass of the world*, London, 1949, 205–18.

——, "Land use within the Common Market", *Economic Geography*, 35, 1959, 1–24.

——, "An evaluation of the standard of land use in Western Europe", *Economic Geography*, 36, 1960, 283–95.

J. Vernant, *The refugee in the post-war world*, London, 1953.

P. Waller, H. S. Swain, "Changing patterns of oil transportation and refining in West Germany", *Economic Geography*, 43, 1967, 143–56.

H. C. Wallich, "Mainspring of the German revival", *Yale Studies in Economics*, 5, 1955.

M. J. Wise, "The Common Market and the changing geography of Europe", *Geography*, 48, 1963, 129–38.

E. Wiskemann, *Germany's eastern neighbours*, London, 1956.

E. M. Yates, "The development of the Rhine", *Institute of British Geographers, Transaction and Papers*, 32, 1963, 65–81.

References to Regions
THE NORTH-WEST

R. Barrington, "The Hamburg 'outer harbour' project and related developments", *Tijdschrift voor Economische en Sociale Geografie*, 59, 1968, 106–8.

J. Bird, "Seaports and the European Economic Community", *Geographical Journal*, 133, 1967, 302–27.

C. Degn, U. Muss, *Luftbildatlas Schleswig-Holstein*, Neumünster, 1965.

——, *Topographischer Atlas Schleswig-Holstein*, Neumünster, 1966.

R. E. Dickinson, "The Braunschweig industrial area", *Economic Geography*, 34, 1958, 249–63.

Gesellschaft für Wirtschaftsförderung Bremen (ed.), *Bremen—Bremerhaven. Häfen am Strom—River Weser Ports*, Bremen, 1964.

T. Green, "Hanover, Kiel and Cologne. Post-war reconstruction and design", *Tijdschrift voor Economische en Sociale Geografie*, 52, 1961, 85–94.

F. W. Morgan, "The pre-war hinterlands of the German North Sea ports", *Institute of British Geographers, Transactions and Papers*, 14, 1948, 43–55.

E. Schrader, *Die Landschaften Niedersachsens* [atlas], Hanover, 1957.

K. A. Sinnhuber, "German sea fishing", *Geography*, 39, 1954, 35–7.

G. G. Weigend, "The functional development of the port of Hamburg", *Tijdschrift voor Economische en Sociale Geografie*, 47, 1956, 113–20.

——, "The problem of hinterland and foreland as illustrated by the port of Hamburg", *Economic Geography*, 32, 1956, 1–16.

NORTHERN RHINELAND AND WESTPHALIA

J. Barr, "Planning for the Ruhr", *Geographical Magazine*, 42, 1970, 280–9.

R. E. Dickinson, "Cologne", in *City and Region*, London, 1964, 265–73.

T. H. Elkins, "The Cologne brown coal field", *Institute of British Geographers, Transactions and Papers*, 19, 1953, 131–43.

——, "An English traveller in the Siegerland", *Geographical Journal*, 122, 1956, 306–16.

—— and E. M. Yates, "Lower Berg; a distinctive region between Rhine and Ruhr", *Geography*, 43, 1958, 104–14.

D. K. Fleming, G. Krumme, "The 'Royal' Hoesch Union", *Tijdschrift voor Economische en Sociale Geografie*, 49, 1968, 177–99.

P. Hall, "Rhine-Ruhr", in *The world cities*, London, 1966, 122–57.

A. Harris, W. Matzot, "Developments in the Aachen coalfield", *Geography*, 44, 1959, 122–4.

J. Körber, "Planning research in the Federal Republic of Germany, with special reference to the Ruhr area", *Journal of the Town Planning Institute*, 52, 1966, 131–3.

N. J. Pounds, "The Ruhr area; a problem of definition", *Geography*, 36, 1951, 165–78.

——, *The Ruhr; a study in historical and economic geography*, London, 1952.

——, "The localisation of the iron and steel industry in north-west Germany", *Tijdschrift voor Economische en Sociale Geografie*, 42, 1951, 174–81.

Siedlungsverband Ruhrkohlenbezirk (ed.), *Regionalplanung* [atlas], Essen, 1960.

THE MIDDLE RHINE HIGHLANDS AND THE HESSE AND WESER HILLS

K. L. Borbief, "The rebuilt centres of Hanover and Kassel", *Journal of the Town Planning Institute*, 45, 1959, 59–61.

R. Common, "Central Hesse", *Oriental Geographer*, 9, 1965, 41–62.

T. H. Elkins and E. M. Yates, "The Neuwied basin", *Geography*, 45, 1960, 39–51.

A. Kühn (ed.), Land Hessen [atlas], *Deutscher Planungsatlas*, 4, Bremen, 1960.

B. Little, "Trier, Germany's oldest city", *Geographical Magazine*, 34, 1961, 169–79.

G. Schofield, "The canalization of the Moselle", *Geography*, 50, 1965, 161–3.

THE SOUTH GERMAN SCARP AND VALE COUNTRY

H. G. Barnum, "Market centers and hinterlands in Baden-Württemberg", *University of Chicago, Department of Geography, Research Paper*, 103, Chicago, 1966.

D. Burtenshaw, "Recent changes in Saar coalmining", *Geography*, 53, 1968, 404–6.

T. H. Elkins, E. M. Yates, "The south German scarpland in the vicinity of Tübingen", *Geography*, 48, 1963, 372–92.

C. C. Held, "The new Saarland", *Geographical Review*, 41, 1951, 590–605.

A. F. A. Mutton, "Place names and the history of settlement in S.W. Germany", *Geography*, 23, 1938, 113–19.

H. Overbeck, G. W. Sante, *Saar-Atlas*, Gotha, 1934.

R. S. Platt, "The Saarland, an international borderland", *Erdkunde*, 15, 1961, 54–68.

THE GERMAN ALPS AND THEIR FORELAND

A. Kühn (ed.), Bayern [atlas], *Deutscher Planungsatlas*, 5, Bremen, 1960.

A. F. A. Mutton, A. E. Adams, "Land forms, settlement and land utilisation in the southern Allgäu", *Economic Geography*, 15, 1939, 169–78.

GERMANY EAST OF THE ELBE–SAALE LINE

H. Aubin, "The lands east of the Elbe and German colonisation eastwards", in *Cambridge Economic History*, I, Cambridge, 1928, 361–92.

W. Krallert, *Atlas zur Geschichte der deutschen Ostsiedlung*, Bielefeld, 1958.

T. Kraus (and others), *Atlas östliches Mitteleuropa*, Bielefeld, 1959. [With comprehensive bibliography and a key in German, English and French.]

F. W. Morgan, "The pre-war hinterlands of the German Baltic ports", *Geography*, 34, 1949, 201–11.

MIDDLE GERMANY

W. Behrmann (ed.), Atlas von Berlin, *Deutscher Planungsatlas*, 9, Bremen, 1960.

H. Busch, *German Democratic Republic; Outline*, Dresden, 1967.

D. Childs, "Recent East German economic progress", *Geography*, 51, 1966, 367–9.

Department of State (ed.), "Berlin, city between two worlds" *European and British Commonwealth Series*, 61, Washington, D.C., 1960.

R. E. Dickinson, "Mitteldeutschland; the middle Elbe basin as a geographical unit", *Geographical Journal*, 103, 1944, 211–25.

T. H. Elkins, "East Germany's brown coal industry", *Geography*, 41, 1956, 192–5.

——, "The Central German chemical industry", *Geography*, 42, 1957, 183–6.

——, "West and East Berlin in 1959", *Geography*, 45, 1959, 268–71.

——, "East Germany's new industrial plan", *Geography*, 45, 1960, 217–20,

——, "The economic background to Berlin", *Geography*, 47, 19, 62, 92–5.

——, "Both sides of Berlin", *Geographical Magazine*, 41, 1969, 382–92.

F. Friedensburg, "The geographical elements in the Berlin situation", *Geographical Journal*, 133, 1967, 137–47.

D. J. Irving, *The destruction of Dresden*, London, 1963.

Her Majesty's Government (ed.), *The meaning of Berlin*, London, 1962.

R. Matz, *Agrar Atlas über das Gebiet der D.D.R.*, Gotha, 1956.

R. E. H. Mellor, "The German Democratic Republic's falling population", *Geography*, 47, 1962, 409–12.

——, "A minority problem in Germany", *Scottish Geographical Magazine*, 79, 1963, 49–53.

G. W. S. Robinson, "West Berlin, the geography of an enclave", *Geographical Review*, 43, 1953, 540–57, also in H. J. de Blij, *Systematic Political Geography*, New York, 1967, 48–65.

O. Schlüter, O. August, *Atlas des Saale—und mittleren Elbegebietes*, Leipzig, 1958–61.

K. A. Sinnhuber, "Eisenhüttenstadt and other new industrial locations east of Berlin", *Festschrift Leopold G. Scheidl*, Wien, 1965, 328–48.

Staatliche Zentralverwaltung für Statistik, *Statistical pocket book of the German Democratic Republic*, Berlin [East], annually.

United States Information Service, *Berlin—1961. The background*, London, 1961.

University of Sydney, Department of Tutorial Classes, "Berlin pressure point", *Current Affairs Bulletin*, 26, 1962, 131–44.

——, "Berlin west of the wall", *Current Affairs Bulletin*, 31, 1963, 66–80.

Verlag Zeit im Bild (ed.), *A little journey through the G.D.R.*, Dresden, 1967.

THE EAST

F. Burda (ed.), *Jenseits von Oder und Neisse*, Offenburg, 1965 [a pictorial account mostly in colour].

E. van Cleef, "East Baltic ports and boundaries, with special reference to Königsberg", *Geographical Review*, 35, 1945, 257–72.

G. Conzen, "East Prussia; some aspects of its historical geography", *Geography*, 30, 1945, 1–10.

R. Hartshorne, "The Upper Silesian industrial district", *Geographical Review*, 24, 1939, 42–8.

M. Kornilowicz (ed.), *Western and northern Poland*, Poznan, 1962.

B. Kortus, "Comparative analysis of industrial regions: the Donbass and Upper Silesia", *Geographia Polonica*, 2, 1964, 183–92.

L. Kosinski, "Problems of settling the Polish western and northern territories", *Polish Geographical Review*, 32, 1960, supplement, 193–209.

——, "Demographic problems of the Polish western and northern territories", in N. J. G. Pounds (ed.), *Geographical Essays on Eastern Europe, Russian and East European Institute, Indiana University Publications*, 24, Bloomington, 1961, 28–53.

——, "Demographical problems of the Polish western territories", *Information Bulletin*, 7, Poznan, 1965.

W. Maas, "The 'Dutch' villages in Poland", *Geography*, 36, 1951, 263–8.

R. E. H. Mellor, "The present situation in East Prussia", *Geography*, 39, 1954, 204–6.

J. Mikolajski, "Polish sea ports, their hinterlands and forelands", *Geographia Polonica*, 2, 1964, 221–9.

N. J. G. Pounds, "The Upper Silesian industrial region", *Russian and East European Series, Russian and East European Institute, Indiana University Publications*, 11, Bloomington, 1958.

——, "The spread of mining in the coal basin of Upper Silesia and northern Moravia", *Annals of the Association of American Geographers*, 48, 1958, 149–63.

B. C. Reece, *On German provinces east of Oder–Neisse line, and economic historical, legal, and political aspects involved*. United States Government Printing Office, Washington, D.C., 1957. [Also in the journal, *Internationales Recht und Diplomatie*, 1957, 126–63.]

K. Saysse-Tobiczyk, *In western Pomerania*, Warsaw, 1963.

A. A. Scholz, *Silesia yesterday and today*, The Hague, 1964.

A. Werwicki, "Changes in the basic functions of towns in Lower Silesia and their influence on urban development", *Geographia Polonica*, 3, Warsaw, 1964, 125–35.

A. Wrzosek, "Change in the spatial structure of Industry in Upper Silesia in 1946–1960", *Geographia Polonica*, 2, 1964, 197–204.

Colour Plates

The North-West

Man's activity has caused a greater variation in the landscape of the North-West than that due to natural differences alone. The photographs illustrate two facets of the city of Hanover, the capital of Lower Saxony: its past in the Baroque garden of the former royal residence, Herrenhausen, and a pedestrian precinct of the new Hanover that has risen from the ruins since 1945.

In the last twenty years the population of West Germany has increased from about 40 millions to nearly 60 millions, mainly resulting from the influx of expellees and refugees. This factor, the replacement of bombed housing, general urban renewal, and movement from city centres, have all given rise to a boom in house building. No fewer than half a million homes a year are now built, a figure comparable with that of the turn of the century, though their standard of design is now much higher.

Blocks of flats characterise post-war building, as this view of the "dormitory settlement", Neue Vahr near Bremen, shows. In the past shortage of space within city walls necessitated high building. This reason no longer applies, but tradition, a harsher climate than in Britain and the resulting higher construction costs discourage the building of individual houses on the outskirts of cities.

Nearly a third of the homes built today are financed by non-profit-making housing associations. By the end of 1965, one of the largest of these, Neue Heimat (New Home) had built 240,000; of this number, 10,000 are to be found in the settlement shown.

The Lower Rhine Bay...

Most people connect the Ruhr with coal mining. True, pit-head structures are still a dominant feature, but on many derricks the wheels have ceased to turn. Mines which have become uneconomic are closing. These include some of the largest with the most modern equipment, like the Bismarck mine shown here. Brown coal has not yet suffered a recession where, as happens to the west of Cologne, it occurs in sufficient quantities near enough to the surface to be mined in huge open pits. Though less disturbed than the Ruhr coal seams, the brown coal seams were also faulted and the picture of the edge of one of these gigantic pits shows one of these faults. Although modern mining operations allow extraction from greater depths, vast deposits lie deeper than the economic limit. Until quite recently coal and brown coal were important raw materials in many processes in the manufacture of chemicals. Chemical plants were therefore located near coalfields or on waterways, as for example the Bayer plant at Leverkusen (founded in 1860) illustrated here. With a labour force of about 25,000 it is now one of the largest chemical works in Germany. Famous for pharmaceuticals, a list of its products would fill a page. Alas, the recent expansion of this "growth industry" was of no benefit to coal, for oil has taken its place as one of the basic raw materials.

...and its Upland Fringe

The traditional West German farm is the owner-occupied family unit. After the war their number greatly declined but the remaining ones are now correspondingly larger. Other improvements of the farming structure which have been made include simplification of the field pattern (Flurbereinigung) and the re-location of some farms away from villages. These new farms are no longer built in the traditional style of the region but are purely functional. This applies also where new farming settlements were created mainly for refugees. An example is the farm shown, located where a war-ravaged forest in the Eifel Mountains was cleared.

The traditional farm illustrated, an example from the Siegerland, is certainly more attractive but would be too costly to build. Siegerland farming used to be closely linked with industry through part-time employment of farm workers in the iron works and by the fact that some of the farmland was a "Hauberg", a plot used alternately as arable land and oak coppice to provide charcoal and tanning bark. This practice has ceased but the importance of woodland in the economy has not diminished. A handicap to efficient forestry is the widespread division of forests into small plots. This can be seen on the right-hand side of the view of northern Sauerland. The small sawmill is equally indicative of this fact.

From the
Harz Mountains...

Despite great contrasts the Moselle Valley and the Harz Mountains have much in common. Both have, for instance, a rich cultural inheritance, in one case based on the veins of precious metals mined since the Middle Ages, in the other arising from the even more ancient cultivation of the vine.

...to the
Moselle Valley

However, while viticulture has been expanding in the Moselle Valley, mining in the Harz Mountains has ceased. Thus a recent source of income common to both is relatively more important for the Harz Mountains— tourism. In this field they have the advantage of offering facilities also for winter sport. In the Moselle valley it is the towns which attract the visitors. A major tourist centre is the town of Cochem; another further upstream which stands supreme as a wine town is Bernkastel (pictured on the right).

There is yet another parallel. Like the reservoirs of the Harz Mountains (one built recently is shown), the dams of the Moselle, though built primarily to make it a modern waterway, are also a source of electricity. Note the slender curved dam which indicates that it is anchored to a very hard rock—it is in fact granite—which will accept the great water pressure transferred to it by a dam of that type.

IV

Between Rhine, Main...

The German Uplands comprise in the heights the dark spruce woodland of the Black Forest, above a lowland of densely settled basins and valleys. The juxtaposition of the two types of area is the keynote of this scarp and vale country.

Of the Frankfurt conurbation, Rüsselsheim on the Main (above left), has become synonymous with the Opel firm, shown in the foreground. Now taking second place amongst Germany's car manufacturers, the firm dates from the pre-car era. The founder-father, Adam Opel, began in 1862 by making sewing machines, and in 1880 turned to the production of bicycles. The first car left the factory in 1898, although for some time bicycles still remained more important. Mass production of cars started in 1924 and since then, apart from the period of World War II and its aftermath, the firm has continued to expand. In 1965 production totalled over 600,000 cars.

The heights of the Uplands, with their dispersed farms, in winter only accessible by ski and sleigh, and their villages and hamlets, constitute quite a different world from the bustle of the valleys. Yet there are various links between them; the heights are areas of recreation for city dwellers, and they make a direct contribution to industrial production in that the lakes—like the Schluchsee (lower) which has been greatly increased in size—are sources of hydroelectric power.

... and Danube

The historical fragmentation of Germany has left its geographical record in, for instance, the many residences of former rulers. An outstanding example is Schloss Ludwigsburg near Stuttgart (opposite). The court theatre and courtyard provide a perfect setting for the schloss concerts and summer festivals. What greater contrast to this splendour could be imagined than the stark utility of the residential accommodation of the Allied Forces. In particular, American blocks of flats with their accompanying schools, shops, etc., form self-contained urban communities, like the "Sky-line" settlement near Würzburg (shown above left).

Many factors combined to make the land between the Rhine, Main and Danube a region of skilled industries. This specialisation became further emphasised after 1945 through the resettlement in this area of expellees and refugees anxious to continue their craft. In some cases a number in the same trade established their homes together and a series of completely new settlements resulted. The foundation stone was laid in 1949 at such a village near Erlangen which specialises in the making of stringed instruments, and the occupation of its inhabitants is illustrated in a fresco on one of the houses (above right).

Despite the absence of heavy industry it was found worthwhile to canalise the Main and Neckar. To reduce delays at locks and to save water the modern type of twin lock is widely used, as the picture of navigation on the Neckar shows. Note the cargo of motor bodies on the barge going downstream (left), as opposed to the bulk commodity one usually associates with inland water transport.

Until the nineteenth century not only the Danube—shown in the lower picture at Ulm—but other rivers of the Alpine Foreland, including the Salzach, were used for navigation, an asset to trading in the cities along their banks. An example of this is Burghausen (above), with its well preserved townscape. Lately a modern quarter has developed as a result of the growth of electrochemical industry and the building of an oil refinery.

The German Alpine Land

The impressive scenery of the Limestone Alps, the attractiveness of villages and towns and the friendliness of the people combine to form the German Alpine Land. With the Alpine Chains as a backcloth, the Alpine Foreland and Alps constitute Germany's leading tourist area. Bavaria and Baden-Württemberg which share this region represent together 60 out of the Federal Republic's total of 145 million tourist days per year. The most important resorts, each with more than one million overnight stays a year, are Constance, Oberstdorf in the Allgäu, Garmisch-Partenkirchen, Mittenwald, Berchtesgaden and Bad Reichenhall. A particular attraction of Garmisch, of which a street scene is depicted below, is its location at the foot of Germany's highest mountain-range; in the case of Berchtesgaden, it is its proximity to what is probably the most spectacular vista in the German Alps—the rise of the Watzmann east face, from the shore of the Königssee, of nearly 7,000 feet (pictured left).

From the Mecklenburg Coast...

The hummocky moraine relief was flooded by the postglacial rise of the Baltic and resulted in an irregular coastline with many peninsulas and islands. The waves continue to undercut the moraines and, as they wash away the finer material, give rise to beaches strewn with huge "erratics", boulders carried there from Scandinavia by the Quaternary glaciers. This is illustrated (far right) by a scene from the island of Hiddensee. Elsewhere sea currents have built up sandspits and linked up formerly separate islands. Rügen is the classic example of such a composite island; Rügen's fame rests, however, on its white chalk cliff shown here, the "Königsstuhl", one of the few instances where solid rock comes to the surface in the Northern Lowland. All these islands and the sandy coastal stretches of the mainland are a great attraction for summer visitors, as also is the convenient link to Sweden; a causeway has been built carrying a railway to Sassnitz on Rügen from where a twice-daily rail ferry goes to Trelleborg in Sweden. (Sassnitz is also an important fishing port of the G.D.R.)

Along the coast of the mainland a number of ports developed in the Middle Ages at sheltered anchorages. One of particular importance was the Hanseatic city of Rostock on the Warnow River (shown here). However, the use of the old harbour in the picture is soon to cease in favour of the modern "Ocean Harbour" at the mouth of the Warnow. Note the postwar buildings where an attempt has been made to build in the Hanseatic tradition, and also the "Neptune" shipyard just behind the steeple.

X

....to the Lusatian Heights

In "Socialist" Germany, possession and running of a motor car is still a luxury only a minority can afford and no rapid change of this situation is to be expected. However, for the lucky few and for the visitor from abroad, motoring on the greatly underused motorways can be a real pleasure, even if the road surface is not as good as in the West. The empty motorway, still with its pre-war road surface, shown here (far left) was photographed at noon in 1965 on the Berlin–Frankfurt–on–Oder autobahn.

A greater proportion of car owners is to be found in areas where key industries were built up from scratch or have greatly expanded, for compared with others, workers in such industries are well paid. One of these places is Eisenhüttenstadt, the iron smelting town—as its name implies. Its main street, Lenin Avenue, which runs from the Party Headquarters to the entrance of the iron works, is lined by well stocked modern shops including a car showroom. Note the blast furnace—one of six—in the background and the modern building style of the point blocks in the foreground, a pleasant change from the sham "Stalinesque" of earlier years.

In Southern Brandenburg the greatest change has been the vast increase in the mining of brown coal, largely for use in giant power stations. The most recent of these is Vetschau, seen in its rural setting (above left) which, together with another previously built at Lübbenau, produced in 1967 about a quarter of the Democratic Republic's annual total of electricity.

Saxony – Tradition and Progress

Two features of the architectural landscape reflect the geographical character of Saxony: the physical expressions of an important cultural tradition, its theatres, concert halls and, most outstanding, the exquisite Baroque architecture of Dresden and the modern industrial structures, especially of the rapidly expanding chemical industry. Although many of Dresden's famous buildings and art treasures perished in the holocaust that befell the city in 1945, there survived (or were restored) a sufficient number to retain its attraction as the city of the German Democratic Republic visited by the greatest number of tourists.

The most famous of Dresden's buildings is the Zwinger (shown here) which, happily, it was possible to restore. Built in the early eighteenth century it was meant to enclose the outer courtyard of a huge palace, though, alas, this was never built.

When thinking of industrial plants in Saxony the first that comes to mind is the Leuna Werke. Built originally in 1916/17 to produce nitrogen for the ammunitions industry, it experienced a great expansion before World War II when its main purpose became the production of synthetic petrol and lubricants from brown coal. With a labour force of nearly 30,000 it is the largest industrial plant in the "Soviet Zone". Close by, a new chemical plant, Leuna II, is in process of construction and has started production. Completion is scheduled for 1970. Instead of brown coal, oil is its main raw material; when completed the plant is expected to be, in terms of output per worker, ten times as efficient as Leuna I.

Between Neisse....

Part of the boundary shared by Silesia and Bohemia is formed by the Giant Mountains, known in Germany as the Riesengebirge and in Poland, Karkonosze. This mountain range, in which it is said a friendly spirit called Rübezahl used to appear to the lonely wanderer, rises higher than any other of the German Uplands (to over 5,000 feet), to reach above the tree line. With mountain scenery formed by Ice Age glaciers at the highest points and good snow conditions in winter, it became the favourite holiday resort for thousands of Berliners. But now, separated from this source of its main stream of tourists by the Oder-Neisse frontier, many of its Bauden, the tourist chalets which had developed from the summer huts of the herdsmen, have passed out of use and fallen into disrepair. The decline of the tourist trade is also evident in the pitiful state of some of the former resorts.

Ruined buildings are not, however, confined to these instances but are still widespread in many other towns and villages of Silesia. Most are the result of the War but there are also many cases, especially in the smaller towns, where buildings, although bearing the official Polish plaque of "Protected Ancient Monument", have been allowed through neglect to reach a state beyond repair.

Against this must be set the excellent restoration work done in some of the larger towns and cities. The view showing the façades of restored burghers' houses in the Neumarkt—despite its name, an ancient market square of Breslau—testifies to this.

.... Oder ....

If the **Oder-Neisse Line** really followed the former river as far as its mouth, nearly all of Stettin (Szczecin) would still be inhabited by Germans, for the bulk of the city lies on the western bank; as it is, they form only about half of one per cent of its 315,000 inhabitants. At the end of the War, the city centre lay almost completely in ruins. Much has been achieved since then, but even in 1967 reconstruction was far from complete (the picture dates from 1965). Some of the important public buildings of this former Hanseatic city have been restored; for instance the old town hall (German: Rathaus; Polish: Ratusz) which is the building with the tower behind the blocks of flats under construction. Its main religious building, however, St. Jacob's church (in the foreground), is still an empty shell and an open gap separates the east choir from the western section. Although in the town war damage is thus still much in evidence, the harbour installations have not only been rehabilitated but were even expanded. Owing to its advantage of being the most westerly amongst the ports serving Poland, as early as the mid-1950s it became the most important. In 1966 its turnover had reached nearly 11.5 million tons compared with Gdynia's 8.7 and Danzig's (Gdansk) 6.6 million tons.

Prussia was, in the original sense, the land on the Baltic once inhabited by the warrior tribe of the Pruzzi, a people akin to the inhabitants of Latvia and Livonia, and not by Poles or even Slavs. German settlement in Prussia began with the foundation of the Cistercian monastery at Oliva near Danzig in 1170, at about the same time as German merchants established a trading station. After the granting of its charter in 1224, this became the city of Danzig. Shortly afterwards the Order of Teutonic Knights was called upon to be the ally of a Polish ruler against the Pruzzi, and came to this area to Christianise and conquer. The seat of the Grand Master of the Order was Marienburg (Our Lady's Castle— in Polish, Malbork), the largest German castle ever built. Badly damaged towards the end of World War II, it has been faithfully restored to its former splendour by Polish architects.

An even greater achievement was the restoration of the "golden city" of Danzig of which in 1945 only charred ruins were left. But now the original old streets and squares have been reconstructed and appear as in the heyday of the city in the sixteenth and seventeenth centuries. The picture shows the "Long Market" and the town hall which in 1945 was reduced to a burnt-out shell.

It is ironic that Poland should make such efforts to restore and even recreate these witnesses to the German heritage in the so-called "regained Polish territories". But it may perhaps in later generations lead to a more objective appreciation than at present of how great the German contribution was in advancing the civilisation of these areas, and contribute to a new understanding between Germans and Poles, both of them representatives of Western European civilisation.

XV

.... and Memel

The only eastern part of the former German Reich that is still virtually inaccessible to visitors is northern East Prussia or—according to its present status within the Soviet Union—Kaliningrad Oblast. Its capital, also called Kaliningrad, when still under its original name of Königsberg, played an important role in German history: it was the seat of the Dukes of Prussia from 1525 to 1618, and from 1701 onwards, when Prussia became a kingdom, it was here that the coronation of the Prussian kings took place; here also the great German philosopher Immanuel Kant taught and died (in 1804).

In 1945, from the end of January until 9 April the city was under siege and finally taken by the Russian forces, by then hardly more than a heap of rubble. In contrast to Poland, the Soviet Union has made no attempt to rebuild the old quarters of the city as they used to be before destruction. The new buildings which have risen are completely divorced from the past and, furthermore, from the region; similarly, the new name of this and other towns and cities expresses a complete break with the past. Apart from the ruins of the Royal Castle in the background, the view here could be a street scene from almost any new urban quarter in the Soviet Union. However, in addition to the castle, there remain other traces of its German past, including for instance the Schiller monument (though the poet's name is now given also in Cyrillic letters), the grave of Kant, the playhouse, the main railway station and the grain elevators of the port. From the limited information available, it appears, however, that this townscape has almost entirely lost its German character.

Index